Why Leaders
Can't Lead

Why Leaders
Can't Lead

The Unconscious Conspiracy Continues

WARREN BENNIS

Jossey-Bass Publishers
San Francisco • London • 1989

WHY LEADERS CAN'T LEAD
The Unconscious Conspiracy Continues
  by Warren Bennis

Library of Congress Cataloging-in-Publication Data

Bennis, Warren
  Why leaders can't lead.

  (The Jossey-Bass management series)
  Includes index.
  1. Leadership. 2. Social change. 3. Civilization,
Modern—20th century. 4. United States—Civilization—
20th century. 5. United States—Social conditions—
1980-   . I. Title. II. Series.
HM141.B434   1989   303.3'4   88-46091
ISBN 1-55542-152-0 (alk. paper)

Manufactured in the United States of America

The paper in this book meets the guidelines for
permanence and durability of the Committee on
Production Guidelines for Book Longevity of the
Council on Library Resources.

JACKET DESIGN BY WILLI BAUM

FIRST EDITION

Code 8927

The Jossey-Bass
Management Series

Consulting Editors
Organizations and Management

WARREN BENNIS
University of Southern California

RICHARD O. MASON
Southern Methodist University

IAN I. MITROFF
University of Southern California

Contents

Preface

Twelve years ago, I wrote *The Unconscious Conspiracy: Why Leaders Can't Lead.* It stirred up a bit of a commotion at the time. I was pleased to learn last summer that university presidents had named it (along with a more recent book of mine—*Leaders* [1985]) as one of their favorite books on leadership. I was pleased and disturbed, actually, since its continuing popularity suggests that while the players have changed, as the world has, their predicament has not—except perhaps for the worse. In America today, it is harder than ever to lead. One of my favorite social barometers, the bumper sticker, corroborates this. There has been a resurgence lately of such exhortations as "Don't Vote—It Will Only Encourage Them." For at least the second time, "Impeach Someone" is popular. Though we need leaders as much as ever, we have never held them in lower regard. Circumstances conspire against them. And so—without meaning to—do the American people.

Writers and teachers like to think that once they have identified a problem and offered some solutions, the problem is on its way to being solved. Having named the leadership problem in 1976, and having pointed out the direction in which I thought solutions might lurk, I moved on to fresh pastures. One such verdant field was an extensive study of leaders and the characteristics of leadership, which (with my coauthor Burt Nanus) I described in *Leaders.*

My next project was to have been a book titled *Managing the Dream,* in which I planned to focus on the application of leadership, spotlighting a variety of leaders and their organizations. As often happens, however, I had to go back before I could go forward. I needed to look again at the context of leadership—at our organizations and at society itself—because leaders do not emerge from or function in a vacuum, and there has never been a more challenging context than the one in which we live today.

My intent at that juncture was simply to update *The Unconscious Conspiracy* to reflect the changed circumstances. Almost immediately, however, I saw that much more was needed. In tone and temper, the 1980s are totally different from the 1970s. Indeed, the 1980s are less an extension of the 1970s than they are the *result* of both the 1960s and the 1970s. In the 1960s, we wanted to make the world better. In the 1970s, we wanted only to make ourselves better. Now, at the close of the 1980s, we seem to be uncertain about whether we can make anything better.

The business world is turbulent, its waters roiled by scandals and a recent stock market crash. The political world is in upheaval, rocked by secret arms deals with terrorists and concessions to foreign despots who deal in drugs and have only contempt for the concept of human rights. The very fabric of our society is being unraveled by unchecked crime and drug traffic, increasing poverty and illiteracy, and unprecedented cynicism toward possible solutions. Who's in charge here? The answer seems to be, no one.

An unconscious conspiracy in contemporary society prevents leaders—no matter what their original vision—from taking charge and making changes. Within any organization, an entrenched bureaucracy with a commitment to the status quo undermines the unwary leader. To make matters worse, certain social forces—the increasing tension between individual rights and the common good, for example—discourage the emergence of leaders. The narcissistic children of the Me Decade seem unwilling to embrace any vision but their own—a narrow one that excludes the possibility of sacrificing a little bit today to gain something better tomorrow. A corollary of this unwillingness to sacrifice is an unwillingness to cooperate with neighbors. Americans are now going through a self-imposed isolation phase: Each individual feels helpless to affect anything beyond the immediate environment and so retreats into an ever-contracting private world—a phenomenon that manifests itself among the affluent as "cocooning" and among the poor as drug addiction. Activism is on the decline, including the simplest form of activism—voting. People float, but they don't dream. And people without a dream are less easily inspired by a leader's vision.

So the bad news is, the arena in which leadership is exercised has deteriorated. The good news is, we have, I believe, a better grasp of the problems and a better sense of the solutions than we did a dozen years ago. In fact, the last third of this new book is devoted to solutions—or parts of a solution. These suggestions for change—and that is really what they are—have been wrung both from my observations of other leaders and from my own years of painful experience.

Why Leaders Can't Lead is an analysis of the problems facing anyone who tries to take charge of an organization—of whatever kind—and effect change. The book offers those engaged in the day-to-day tasks of leadership specific suggestions—not only on how to counter the turmoil and inertia that threaten the best-laid plans, but also on how to keep *routine*, which absorbs time and energy like a sponge, from sapping their ability to make a real impact.

The book is not overly optimistic. But I do think change is possible—even change for the better. Change begins slowly, however, as, one by one, individuals make the conscious choice to live up to their potential.

So *Why Leaders Can't Lead* is intended for everyone in a position of leadership, or aspiring to such a position; for all those concerned with who is elected, promoted, or appointed to leadership in any kind of organization. It is meant for anyone who holds a government office; anyone in public service. It is addressed also to professors of business, political science, and public administration; all department heads, deans, administrators, presidents, and chancellors of universities. It is intended for anyone interested in the future of this society. It will help the reader understand the problems facing leaders in this increasingly complex world of ours. At the same time, it will give leaders some practical ideas on how to deal with the troublesome issues that we all face.

Some material is reprinted here from my earlier book on the subject with very few modifications. The story of Charles Johnson, told in the first chapter, is still a moving example of how pressures from competing constituencies—pressures that are pervasive in our society—can destroy a leader. In the second chapter I retell the tale of the experience at the University of Cincinnati that led me to believe that existing academic theories of leadership were useless; but here the story serves to introduce my subsequent research and the four competencies that I believe are crucial for genuine leadership.

Most of the material in Part Two, "A Society Without Dreams," and Part Three "Parts of the Problem," is new, the results of my reexamination of the context of leadership. Part Four, "Parts of the Solution," is a combination of old and new thoughts. "Quitting on Principle" has been updated, for example, although the issue itself is no different: The analysis is still the best I have to offer of this continuing problem, and I believe the insights are still valid. On the other hand, "Leading to Make a Difference," an essay on choosing self-fulfillment despite the efforts of parents, schools, and organizations to conspire against us, is entirely new, as are some of the other chapters.

This, then, is not *The Unconscious Conspiracy Revised* or even *The Unconscious Conspiracy—The Sequel,* or *Part Two.* This is largely a new book. While my description of our current circumstances may seem grim, I hope it will make the reader aware of the possibilities for change. In fact, I hope it will spur the reader on to take responsibility for change. Abraham Maslow said, "Each time one takes responsibility, this is an actualizing of the self." It is also the first step in taking charge, in becoming a leader.

The best hope I have for this book is that twelve years from now I will look back on it and muse, "Where have all the leaders come from?"

Acknowledgments

My thanks go first of all to William Hicks at Jossey-Bass, for his editorial help and constant knack of making it all seem easy. As for the writing and the ideas behind it, I want to thank Peggy Clifford not only for the prodding and hard work that went into the difficult job of revision but also for her originality of thought. Finally, and most important, a long, deep bow to Judith Garwood, whose "fine Italian hand" is seen throughout and who brought whatever grace and elegance this book contains to every page her gifted hands touched.

Santa Monica, California   Warren Bennis
January 1989

To Douglas McGregor,
whose contribution to the field
and to me, personally,
remains peerless

The Author

Warren Bennis is Distinguished Professor of Business Administration at the University of Southern California. He received his
A.B. degree (1951) from Antioch College in economics and psychology, an Honor Certificate (1952) from the London School
of Economics, and his Ph.D. degree (1955) from the Massachu-
setts Institute of Technology (M.I.T.) in economics and social
science. Bennis served several years on the faculty of the M.I.T.
Sloan School of Management and succeeded Douglas McGregor
as chairman of the Organization Studies Department in the
Sloan School. He has also served as a faculty member at both
Harvard University and Boston University; as provost and executive vice-president of the State University of New York, Buffalo; and as president of the University of Cincinnati (from
1971 to 1977).

Bennis has authored fifteen books and over five hundred
articles. His latest book, *Leaders: The Strategies for Taking
Charge* (1985, with B. Nanus), was cited as the best business
book of the year by Harvard L'Expansion. Twice he has won
the coveted McKinsey Foundation Annual Prize for the best
book on management: in 1967 for *The Professional Manager* and
again in 1968 for *The Temporary Society*. His writings have ap-

peared in the *New York Times, Esquire,* the *Atlantic Monthly,* the *Saturday Review, Psychology Today,* the *Los Angeles Times,* and the *Harvard Business Review.* He is on the board of editors for the *Journal of Creative Behavior,* the *International Journal of Small Group Research,* the *Journal of Occupational Behaviour, Consultation,* the *Journal of Higher Education,* the *Journal of Managerial Psychology,* the *Journal of Humanistic Psychology,* and the *Journal for Higher Education Management.* He is also a consulting editor for the Jossey-Bass Management Series and chairman of the board of editors for the University of Southern California's magazine for executives, *New Management.*

Bennis has been U.S. Professor of Corporations and Society at the Centre d'Etudes Industrielles in Geneva; scholar-in-residence for several years at the Aspen Institute of Humanistic Studies; professor at the Management Development Institute (IMEDE), Lausanne, Switzerland; visiting professor and project director of the Indian Institute of Management in Calcutta, India; Raoul de Vitry D'Avaucourt Professor at INSEAD in Fontainebleau, France; and Distinguished Scholar-in-Residence (1984) at Southern Methodist University.

Bennis has recently been a consultant to Rockwell International, Southern California Gas Company, Equitable Life Assurance, Chase Manhattan Bank, and American Medical International (AMI), where he was instrumental in the establishment of their Corporate College for senior management. He has also acted as a consultant to McKinsey and Company, TRW, Polaroid, and Ford Motor Company and served in an advisory capacity to four U.S. presidents.

Currently, Bennis serves on the boards of directors for First Executive Corporation, the Foothill Group, the California School of Professional Psychology, Transformational Technologies, Inc., the Public Justice Foundation, and the American Leadership Forum, as well as on the advisory boards of the Centre for Managing the Self (Geneva), the American Sports Institute, and Index Systems, Inc. He has also served on the National Advisory Board of the U.S. Chamber of Commerce and the board of the American Management Association.

Warren Bennis has received several honorary degrees. He was awarded the 1987 Dow Jones Award by the American Assembly of Collegiate Schools of Business, for "outstanding contributions and distinguished service to the field of collegiate education for business management." In December 1986, he won the Speaker of the Year Award presented by the American Society for Training and Development, Los Angeles, for "the unusual scope and magnitude of his contribution to the field of HRD, both theory and practice." He has also been the recipient of the Employment Management Association's Pericles Award (1987); University Associates' First Annual Distinguished Contribution Award (1986); the Perry L. Rorher Consulting Practice Award (1983), presented by the American Psychology Association for "demonstrating outstanding ability in applying psychological knowledge and skills to assist organizations to respond more effectively to the challenges of society"; and the Distinguished Service Award (1973), the highest honor accorded by the American Board of Professional Psychologists.

Bennis's pioneering work in the dynamics of organizations has been widely acclaimed. The results of his extensive studies of public and private executives and gifted entrepreneurs who make things happen in America are published in his book *Leaders: The Strategies for Taking Charge* (1985, with B. Nanus).

Why Leaders
Can't Lead

PART ONE

THE UNCONSCIOUS CONSPIRACY AND HOW TO CONFOUND IT

1

One Job, One Year, One Life

At 8:20 A.M. on June 17, 1969, one day after his last ordeal as acting president of the University of Oregon, Dr. Charles Johnson rounded a sharp, blind curve and drove his Volkswagen head-on into a Mack B-61 diesel log truck and Peerless log trailer with a load of thirteen logs weighing sixteen tons. Johnson died instantly. He was forty-eight.

Johnson's body was so mutilated that not even his closest associates could identify him with certainty. Many thought he had committed suicide. They said: "He was depressed." "Everybody knows it." "I heard it on the radio." "Just ask anybody." "He always took the easy way out. He always caved in to student demands. His suicide was just one more easy way out." James Jensen, the president of Oregon State University, said something else: "This is a terrible tragedy. I hope now the people of Oregon will understand. . . ." He paused. "Well, perhaps I'd just better not say what I hope the people of Oregon will understand."

The county medical investigator ruled the death an accident. The curve was a difficult turn that had to be made very carefully, and the sun had been in Johnson's eyes. A psychiatrist who had seen Johnson several days earlier felt that the cause

3

was "partial dissociation, a situational depression caused possibly by some recent campus crisis." Johnson was also weak from a recent bout with Asian flu. And he was known to be an erratic driver. All that we know with any certainty is that many in Oregon, and especially those connected with the University of Oregon, shared after the fact a morbid sense of collective guilt.

Four years after Johnson's death, Ken Metzler (1973) published *Confrontation: The Destruction of a College President*, a faithful chronicle of one year in the life of a university president. Metzler had been an associate professor of journalism at the University of Oregon (UO) and editor of its alumni magazine. He had also served as a secretary to the presidential search committee, which, six weeks before the acting president's death, after excruciatingly intense and erratic deliberations, had finally passed over Johnson, the favorite of many, to choose a former University of Oregon dean, Robert D. Clark, then president of San Jose State University.

Reading the book some years removed from the acrid stench of the Kent State and Jackson State tragedies is an eerie experience. The problems now facing higher education seem so different, so businesslike—they are concerned with fiscal viability, affirmative action for blacks and Latinos that seems to translate into quotas for Asians, students more interested in vocational training than education, and other penultimate questions such as "Who benefits from higher education?" and "Who should pay for it?" Today, college presidents are concerned about the relationship between jobs and education, about growing parsimony at the federal and state levels, and about ways to balance the books. They wince at the memory of the unsystematic growth of the 1950s and 1960s, when most universities (the University of Oregon is a brilliant and bittersweet example) grew and grew like Topsy, proliferating their functions, diffusing their purposes, just doing what came naturally during the two golden decades: operating on margin, very like 1929's speculators. They were hiring four professors on "soft money" (federally supported grants) to every one hired on "hard money" (general funds). They saw graduate education, the indicator of a university's prestige, seriously jeopardized not only by fewer funds (a 40 percent dip in federal fellowships in the sciences alone between 1970 and 1973) but also by fewer students and, worse, fewer jobs. For every four graduate Ph.D.'s in the two decades between 1950 and 1969, three found positions with expanding or new campuses, while only one replaced a professor who had died or retired (see the 1973 Newman Report on Graduate Education). Four years later, in many academic areas, only *one* of four graduating Ph.D.'s would find a job in what he or she was trained for, research and teaching in a university. The situation is no better today.

The problems that Johnson faced during his year as acting president may seem quaint in retrospect; in fact, they were killers. Johnson had to deal in rapid succession with:

• An anemic version of the free-speech movement, which took the form of an outcry about the use of obscenities in the student newspaper.
• A confrontation between two black basketball players who refused to cut their Afros and a new and promising freshman coach who had ordered them to do so, culminating in a demonstration with serious possibilities of violent disruption.
• A dispute concerning the use of California table grapes in the university dining halls.
• Other "brushfires" (Johnson's term) dealing with black students' rights, the bombing and destruction of valuable and expensive ROTC equipment, and similar problems that were then convulsing our fragile institutions of higher learning.

Johnson also inherited a messy fiscal situation from his predecessor, the ebullient former HEW secretary Arthur Flemming, who ran the university for the seven years preceding Johnson's term of office with a "go-go" style of enthusiasm and optimism. Flemming employed a "management by addition" style of leadership, one followed by many public institutions and some private ones in those beamish years in an attempt to compete with the eastern educational establishment.

Johnson comes through as an unpretentious, wry man of dry wit, strong analytical powers, and self-effacing style. He was healthily skeptical of power but at times wanted it more than his words—especially his letters to the folks back home—can conceal. He was straightforward, awkward, homespun. He enjoyed parlor games and rural jokes, he liked spending time with his family, and, most of all, he enjoyed good fun.

He was almost totally inaccessible to his own feelings and, in turn, to other people's feelings. I doubt that Johnson himself or his family would ever have termed him complex, but complex he was, especially in regard to whatever tragic flaw held him in its vise and then slowly released him.

Whatever issue popped up on or careened off the University of Oregon campus in the 1968–69 academic year, Johnson was usually in the middle of it. In the obscenity issue, he was hit with the fallout of the "moderate liberal" reputation of that "highfalutin and gallivantin' politician" Arthur Flemming and was able to secure the respect of at least some members of the academic community by standing on the venerable principle of free speech. The "hair" issue found him optimistically trying somehow to convince the coach to relax his rules or the players to shave off perhaps not the *whole* Afro but possibly an inch or two. Here he was caught in the middle of a "no win" situation. He took the side of the two black players. The promising young coach was ordered to stay home rather than be at the game, and, to make matters worse, the team lost badly. The sports and editorial writers, alumni, public officials, citizenry, and legislators (these last then in session determining the university's budget) were outraged.

Then there was the grape issue. Cesar Chavez's attempts to unionize the migrant grape pickers in California captivated some students, who demanded that the university boycott non-UFW (United Farm Workers) grapes. When the case first came up, Johnson had to ask his daughter, a UO freshman, who Chavez was and what this was all about. Later in the year, he publicly called a halt to the purchasing of grapes for reasons that had little to do with the boycott. In so doing, he infuriated some legislators who were directly involved in marketing grapes.

Johnson sought valiantly to uphold the classic concept of the American university as a citadel of contemplation sheltering all refugees from a "sick society," defending the bastions of ideas against Philistine outrages. In fact, such confrontations make the vaunted bastion appear like little more than the flimsiest scrim, pitifully vulnerable to potshots from the neighboring community. The alumni, the press, the legislators, the general public, the parents, and all those involved in the financial support of the university, through either alumni giving or taxes, escalated their attacks against it. One could wish to report that there was appreciation and generosity within the university regarding Johnson's courageous stands, but more often than not, apart from an infrequent pat on the back or an occasional faculty letter commending his principles, the internal "community" was mute or even "annoyed." The expressions of dissatisfaction from the enraged citizenry were far more strident, shrill, and incessant than could ever be counterbalanced by whatever satisfactions Johnson's decisions had meant for the academic community.

There is no institution more vulnerable to and hence more dependent on external forces than the American university. One reason is the proliferation of sponsored research. I am not suggesting that universities cancel contracts with external sponsors. But conflicts with the mission of the university will inevitably arise. Another reason is that the universities are not self-supporting. Tuition pays only a small percentage of the costs of running a university; most of the rest comes from alumni or, in the case of public universities, the state. The falsely lulling self-image of the university that it is remote and distant and somewhat "above" the outside society that nourishes and feeds it not only is outdated but, if believed and acted on, will bring about the university's destruction.

The "outside" clobbered Johnson. What happened to this thoughtful, high-principled, liberal, and, above all, decent human being? He was so perceptive, so aware of those forces that could destroy him, yet something prevented him from exercising his intellectual mastery before a wise, practical judgment could be made.

Ken Metzler conducted more than 300 interviews, talking to many of Johnson's close friends and relatives. He was fortu-

nate to have in his subject a man who himself faithfully re-
corded his ideas and premonitions and described his own behavior and decisions. Thus we have access to the raw experiences of
a man in crisis. This allows us to employ a variety of analytical
prisms in seeking to explain at least some of the man's behavior
and the events that occurred. I shall attempt to employ a few.

Perhaps the most obvious fact is that Johnson had "psychological problems." He had suffered a number of serious lapses
referred to by his psychiatrist as "dissociative processes" and,
specifically, an episode of fugue one night shortly before his
death, when he had driven two miles and then wandered dazed
in the woods and even into a river without seeming to know
what he had done. This seemed to be partly induced by over-
work, by weakness from his attack of the flu, and doubtless also
by shock and despair over having been passed over for the university presidency—despite his claimed lack of interest in the job.

Johnson's childhood included the early death of his
mother and obvious problems of achievement; somehow he
often managed to just miss his goal ever so slightly. For example,
in military school, his height enabled him to make the basketball team, but he spent most of the season on the bench, de-
jected, head down, until he finally gave it up. He was very interested in the Boy Scouts and attained the near-top status of Life
Scout but stopped just one merit badge short of the top rank,
Eagle Scout. Lofty and strong ambition shows through the self-
depreciation of his gawkiness (he was six feet, four inches tall)
and rural "plain folks" humor. His letters to his parents were
painfully revealing: "Oh, I guess I might allow my name to be
forwarded to the search committee, although the classroom sure
does beckon; teaching is simplicity and I love it. But, still, maybe they'll be 'dumb enough' to accept this old country boy." So
his country-boy manner, partly real, partly feigned, allowed him
to grope backward and upward without ever looking too bad if
he fell in the process. But beneath his humility was a driving,
perfectionist ambition, spurred perhaps by a demanding and
puritanical father, a kind of "number two" syndrome, and considerable grief and loneliness during his youth.

He was a man who embodied the core values of the academy and its institutional imperative, cognitive rationality: the life of the mind, inexorable logic, reliance on numbers and verbal symbols as strategies of truth (for a man who was a CPA and a professor of accounting, it was primarily numbers). This was the very basis of reality for Johnson.

His rationality was confounded in the "hair" episode by irrational, strident voices from outside who expressed its issues in such emotional terms as "knuckling under to those 'colored' folks." How could he respond to letters from all of the "concerned citizens" who questioned his patriotism and attacked him for his lack of firmness, backbone, and discipline? How does one use logic, empiricism, and the fact-finding, democratic process—slow, creaky, and painfully banal in its operation—to compete with the aphrodisia of confrontations where the operative slogan of the most destructive student radicals could be summarized as "Act now, think later!" and where the highest level of response to Johnson's lengthy, patient, and painstakingly clear explanations was a terse and reflexive "Bullshit!"?

Perhaps all this "psychologizing" is irrelevant. Metzler says that Johnson was "the wrong man for the wrong job at the wrong time." Perhaps it was the Peter Principle at work—Johnson's former experience as dean of a college not only did not prepare him for the presidency but may have instilled in him certain principles and guidelines to action that were antithetical to the pneumatic beat of the crises that were continually hammered out on the anvil of Johnson's psyche.

Perhaps it was the times. Who in the world at any major university could have successfully coped with the exquisite pains and pressures of that year of 1968–69? There was no way— in any single case—that Johnson could have planted even a small flag of victory. The best he could do in situation after situation was to minimize damage or danger or loss. And these terrible little irrational brushfires continually interfered with what this accounting professor knew to be, long before others suspected it, a terrible financial overextension of the university. Hoping to reverse it, he would retire to his home whenever he could stay away from his demanding social obligations and, taking his budget to the bedroom, work on it, night after night, alone.

Having lived through that period as an administrator, I find it impossible to second-guess anybody's decisions during that chaotic time. In his commencement talk, Johnson concluded with Dickens's "It was the best of times, it was the worst of times." For those who were in Johnson's shoes in that final year of a decade that started off so beautifully for higher education and ended up so ravaged, one could only say that it was the worst of times.

Perhaps it was Johnson's leadership style. My guess is that it was the "liberal" administrator who had the roughest time. The liberal presidents who began office then included Kenneth Pitzer of Stanford, Morris Abram of Brandeis, Robert Etherington of Wesleyan; all resigned before their second year. I suspect the trouble is in the liberal style—a style of negotiation, of splitting differences, of bringing people together to iron out differences, of sitting down with the coach and the black players and "talking it out." This style could work during a time of shared values, but not in the charged and polarized situation that developed then. It is one thing to negotiate differences when the stakes are only economic, the kinds of things that once brought labor unions and management to the bargaining table. It is another thing to negotiate between morally antithetical viewpoints.

Wanting to demonstrate how the poor had to live, that spring some students started moving old tarpaper shacks onto the front of the beautiful campus lawn. Daily, more and more shacks appeared. How many, if any, should be allowed? Do you ask the students to remove all the shacks except, say, one (in order to demonstrate and amplify the meaning of poverty) and offer in exchange to provide them more courses in social justice and "peaceful or nonviolent means of social change"?

Often Johnson seemed to walk into situations with the belief that he personally could get the opposing sides to reason together to achieve some viable consensus. But how could one bring about reason—much less consensus—among an outraged citizenry, black students striving for their own group identity and consciousness, the sons and daughters of mechanics and farmers who were spending their last dollar to send their children to school, alumni acutely concerned with the slippage of

Oregon's athletic programs, and a faculty devoted to making the University of Oregon competitive with elite universities? Another President Johnson, at the same time, was discovering that Isaiah's wisdom could reach neither Hanoi, Saigon, nor the SDS.

From the analytical prism of a student of organizational behavior, I would say that the university's social organization doesn't provide the adjustive mechanisms of protection and cushioning for the president. (From the empirical prism of a former university president, I would nod in agreement.) It is simply ridiculous to think that the president of a major American corporation would be involved in some of the situations that Johnson found himself in (or that, occasionally, I found myself in). Yet corporation presidents and chairs, like the chief executives of all our institutions, have equivalent nightmares.

An industrial case in point—if, indeed, one is needed—is the story of Eli M. Black, who at 8 A.M. on February 3, 1975, at the age of fifty-three, plunged to his death from the forty-fourth floor of New York's Pan Am Building. Both doors to his office were found bolted from the inside, according to detectives, and a sealed quarter-inch tempered plate glass window had been smashed open—apparently with Black's attache case.

Black had been chair of the United Brands Company, a conglomerate that he had personally built from a small firm making milk-bottle caps to an organization that could take over, first, one of the country's largest meat packers, John Morrell & Company, and, second, the United Fruit Company. United Brands, said the *New York Times*, had incurred heavy losses in Central American banana plantations as a result of Hurricane Fifi, had undergone new burdens with export taxes on bananas imposed by Central American republics, and had sustained losses in its meat-packing division as a result of increased costs of feeding cattle. Family members and business associates of Black suggested that additional business pressures—mainly those connected with the sale of Foster Grant—were responsible for his state of mind, which was "low."

A subsequent investigation by the Securities and Exchange Commission, routinely conducted after the suicide of any top corporate executive, turned up another possible reason for

Black's decision to take his life. According to *Newsweek* (April 21, 1975), the SEC inquiry disclosed that Black had authorized the payment of more than $2 million to government officials in Honduras to obtain a tax reduction on the export of bananas. Moreover, the facts seem to indicate that he must have known of other instances of bribery on the part of the big multinational company during his tenure. Black's closest associates, who knew him as a man who put in mercilessly long hours and spent his limited free time working for various Jewish philanthropies, said that he had been determined to end United's image as a Yankee exploiter. If Black had approved the bribes, they insisted, he must have been under heavy pressure to do so.

What happens to top men and women—and I think that men and women who are new to the burdens of high position are especially vulnerable, because they are trying to prove themselves—is that they end up with a kind of battle fatigue, overworked, acting as police and/or ombudsmen and, what's worse, seriously undermining the legitimacy and effectiveness of the other executives reporting to them. They tend to intervene compulsively, arrogating from loyal and competent subordinates what rightly belongs to them. (As one corporate CEO put it, "If I'm walking on the shop floor, and I see a leak in the dike, I have to stick my finger in it.") Presidents can become burnt-out victims of the Peter Principle while denying the best potential leaders below them the responsibility needed for their own learning and development.

Finally, and most of all, we have to question seriously how much caring all of us can develop for our institutions when they have become the anvil and test of all our society's crises and problems. The universities were perhaps the first to feel the real crunch. Metzler (1973) says that the problem with Johnson was that "he cared too much for the institution." Though it may have seemed that way, I don't think it is "caring too much" when one identifies his own self-esteem with the success of the institution. This in fact causes people to identify so much with their institution that they become indivisible from it, so that the damage done by a rock thrown through a window by an angry student is morally and psychologically identical with the physical hurt of the president, so that the success of the football team against its chief rival is related to how one feels about one's own success. To care about an institution means to create a self-activating life, a life of its own, where there is a possibility for others to understand it and care for it in the face of difficult odds, to make their work have meaning in a humane and democratic manner.

The problem is this: How do we develop a sufficient climate of understanding so that the various publics on whom every present-day institution depends for its support, both financial and moral, as well as the people who take its classes or work in its plants and offices, care about the institution and identify with its destiny? Only when we have done this will the "best and the brightest" manage to succeed. Without caring, the institution wouldn't be a place that any of us would like to be responsible for or preside over anyway.

The threads of legitimacy and responsible authority fray too easily and far too rapidly. American universities underwent an unusual year in 1968, but it would be wrong to think that the lessons they learned the hard way apply only to the academy and to a receding period of past history. They apply to all time and all people and institutions and echo with the fury of the fates that determine their destiny.

2

Learning Some Basic Truisms About Leadership

A moment of truth came to me toward the end of my first ten months as president of the University of Cincinnati. The clock was moving toward four in the morning, and I was still in my office, still mired in the incredible mass of paper stacked on my desk. I was bone weary and soul-weary, and I found myself muttering, "Either I can't manage this place, or it's unmanageable." I reached for my calendar and ran my eyes down each hour, half hour, quarter hour, to see where my time had gone that day, the day before, the month before.

Nobel laureate James Franck has said he always recognizes a moment of discovery by "the feeling of terror that seizes me." I felt a trace of it that morning. My discovery was this: *I had become the victim of a vast, amorphous, unwitting, unconscious conspiracy to prevent me from doing anything whatever to change the university's status quo.* Even those of my associates who fully shared my hopes to set new goals, new directions, and to work toward creative change were unconsciously often doing the most to make sure that I would never find the time to begin. I found myself thinking of a friend and former colleague who had taken over one of our top universities with goals and plans that fired up all those around him and who said when he left a few years later, "I never could get around to doing the things I wanted to do."

This discovery, or rediscovery, led me to formulate what might be called Bennis's First Law of Academic Pseudodynamics: Routine work drives out nonroutine work and smothers to death all creative planning, all fundamental change in the university—or any institution.

These were the illustrations facing me: To start, there were 150 letters in the day's mail that required a response. About 50 of them concerned our young dean of the School of Education, Hendrik Gideonse. His job was to bring about change in the teaching of teachers, in our university's relationship to the public schools and to students in the deprived and deteriorating neighborhood around us. Out of these urban schools would come the bulk of our students of the future—as good or as bad as the schools had shaped them.

But the letters were not about education. They were about a baby, the dean's ten-week-old son. Gideonse felt very strongly about certain basic values. He felt especially so about sex roles, about equality for his wife, about making sure she had the time and freedom to develop her own potentials fully. So he was carrying the baby into his office two days a week in a little bassinet, which he kept on his desk while he did his work. The daily *Cincinnati Enquirer* heard about it, took a picture of Hendrik, baby, and bassinet, and played it on page one. TV splashed it across the nation. And my "in" basket began to overflow with letters that urged his arrest for child abuse or at least his immediate dismissal. My only public comment was that we were a tax-supported institution, and if Hendrik could engage in that form of applied humanism and still accomplish the things we both wanted done in education, then, like Lincoln with Grant's whiskey, I'd gladly send him several new babies for adoption.

Hendrik was, of course, simply a man a bit ahead of his time. Today, his actions would be applauded—maybe even with a Father of the Year award. Then, however, Hendrik and his baby ate up quite a bit of my time.

Also on my desk was a note from a professor, complain-

ing that his classroom temperature was down to sixty-five degrees. Perhaps he expected me to grab a wrench and fix it. A
student complained that we wouldn't give him course credit for
acting as assistant to a city council member. Another was unable to get into the student health center. The teacher at my
child's day school, who attended the university, was dissatisfied
with her grades. A parent complained about four-letter words in
a Philip Roth book being used in an English class. The track
coach wanted me to come over to see for myself how bad the
track was. An alumnus couldn't get the football seats he wanted.
Another wanted a coach fired. A teacher had called to tell me
the squash court was closed at 7 P.M. when he wanted to use it.

Perhaps 20 percent of my time that year had been taken
up by a problem at the general hospital, which was city-owned
but administered by the university and served as the teaching
hospital of the university medical school. Some terminal-cancer
patients, with their consent, had been subjected to whole-body
radiation as possibly beneficial therapy. Since the Pentagon saw
this as a convenient way to gather data that might help protect
civilian populations in nuclear warfare, it provided a series of
subsidies for the work.

When this story broke and was pursued in such a way as
to call up comparisons with the Nazis' experiments on human
guinea pigs, it became almost impossible for me or anybody else
to separate the essential facts from the fantasized distortions.
The problem eventually subsided, after a blue-ribbon task force
recommended significant changes in the experiment's design.
But I invested endless time in a matter only vaguely related to
the prime purposes of the university—and wound up being accused by some of interfering with academic freedom.

The radiation experiment and Hendrik's baby illustrate
how the media, particularly TV, make the academic cloister a
goldfish bowl. By focusing on the lurid or the superficial, they
can disrupt a president's proper activities while contributing
nothing to the advancement of knowledge. This leads me to
Bennis's Second Law of Academic Pseudodynamics: Make
whatever grand plans you will, you may be sure the unexpected
or the trivial will disturb and disrupt them.

In my moment of truth, that weary 4 A.M. in my trivia-cluttered office, I began trying to straighten out in my own mind what university presidents should be doing and not doing, what their true priorities should be, how they must lead.

Lead, not *manage:* there is an important difference. Many an institution is very well managed and very poorly led. It may excel in the ability to handle each day all the routine inputs yet may never ask whether the routine should be done at all.

All of us find ourselves acting on routine problems because they are the easiest things to handle. We hesitate to get involved too early in the bigger ones—we collude, as it were, in the unconscious conspiracy to immerse us in routine.

My entrapment in routine made me realize another thing: People were following the old army game. They did not want to take the responsibility for or bear the consequences of decisions they properly should make. The motto was, "Let's push up the tough ones." The consequence was that everybody and anybody was dumping his "wet babies" (as the old State Department hands call them) on my desk, when I had neither the diapers nor the information to take care of them. So I decided that the president's first priority—the sine qua non of effective leadership—was to create an "executive constellation" to run the office of the president. It could be a mixed bag, some vice-presidents, some presidential assistants. The group would have to be compatible in the sense that its members could work together but neither uniform nor conformist—a group of people who knew more than the president about everything within their areas of competency and could attend to daily matters without dropping their wet babies on the president's desk.

What should the president him- or herself do? The president should be a *conceptualist.* That's something more than being just an "idea man." It means being a leader with entrepreneurial vision and the time to spend thinking about the forces that will affect the destiny of the institution. The president must educate board members so that they not only understand the necessity of distinguishing between leadership and management but also can protect the chief executive from getting enmeshed in routine machinery.

Leaders must create for their institutions clear-cut and measurable goals based on advice from all elements of the community. They must be allowed to proceed toward those goals without being crippled by bureaucratic machinery that saps their strength, energy, and initiative. They must be allowed to take risks, to embrace error, to use their creativity to the hilt and encourage those who work with them to use theirs.

These insights gave me the strength to survive my acid test: whether I, as a "leading theorist" of the principles of creative leadership, actually could prove myself a leader. However, the sum total of my experiences as president of the University of Cincinnati convinced me that most of the academic theory on leadership was useless.

After leaving the university, I spent nearly five years researching a book on leadership. I traveled around the country spending time with ninety of the most effective, successful leaders in the nation, sixty from corporations and thirty from the public sector. My goal was to find these leaders' common traits, a task that required more probing than I had expected. For a while, I sensed much more diversity than commonality among them. The group included both left-brain and right-brain thinkers; some who dressed for success and some who didn't; well-spoken, articulate leaders and laconic, inarticulate ones; some John Wayne types and some who were definitely the opposite.

I was finally able to come to some conclusions, of which perhaps the most important is the distinction between leaders and managers: Leaders are people who do the right thing; managers are people who do things right. Both roles are crucial, but they differ profoundly. I often observe people in top positions doing the wrong thing well.

This study also reinforced my earlier insight—that American organizations (and probably those in much of the rest of the industrialized world) are underled and overmanaged. They do not pay enough attention to doing the right thing, while they pay too much attention to doing things right. Part of the fault lies with our schools of management; we teach people how to be good technicians and good staff people, but we don't train people for leadership.

The group of sixty corporate leaders was not especially different from any profile of top leadership in America. The median age was fifty-six. Most were white males, with six black men and six women in the group. The only surprising finding was that all the CEOs not only were still married to their first spouses but also seemed enthusiastic about the institution of marriage. Among the CEOs were Bill Kieschnick, then chair and CEO of Arco, and the late Ray Kroc, of McDonald's.

Public-sector leaders included Harold Williams, who then chaired the Securities and Exchange Commission (SEC); Neil Armstrong, a genuine all-American hero who happened to be at the University of Cincinnati; three elected officials; two orchestra conductors; and two winning athletics coaches. I wanted conductors and coaches because I mistakenly believed that they were the last leaders with complete control over their constituents.

After several years of observation and conversation, I defined four competencies evident to some extent in every member of the group: management of attention; management of meaning; management of trust; and management of self. The first trait apparent in these leaders is their ability to draw others to them, not just because they have a vision but because they communicate an extraordinary focus of commitment. Leaders manage attention through a compelling vision that brings others to a place they have not been before.

One of the people I most wanted to interview was one of the few I could not seem to reach—Leon Fleischer, a well-known child prodigy who grew up to become a prominent pianist, conductor, and musicologist. I happened to be in Aspen, Colorado, one summer while Fleischer was conducting the Aspen Music Festival, and I tried again to reach him, even leaving a note on his dressing-room door. Driving back through downtown Aspen, I saw two perspiring young cellists carrying their instruments, and I offered them a ride to the music tent. They hopped in the back of my jeep, and as we rode I questioned them about

Fleischer. "I'll tell you why he's so great," said one. "He doesn't waste our time."

Fleischer finally agreed not only to be interviewed but to let me watch him rehearse and conduct music classes. I linked the way I saw him work with that simple sentence, "He doesn't waste our time." Every moment Fleischer was before the orchestra, he knew exactly what sound he wanted. He didn't waste time because his intentions were always evident. What united him with the other musicians was their concern with intention and outcome.

When I reflected on my own experience, it struck me that when I was most effective, it was because I knew what I wanted. When I was ineffective, it was because I was unclear about it.

So the first leadership competency is the management of attention through a set of intentions or a vision, not in a mystical or religious sense but in the sense of outcome, goal, or direction.

The second leadership competency is management of meaning. To make dreams apparent to others and to align people with them, leaders must communicate their vision. Communication and alignment work together. Consider, for example, the contrasting styles of Presidents Reagan and Carter. Ronald Reagan is called "the Great Communicator"; one of his speech writers said that Reagan can read the phone book and make it interesting. The reason is that Reagan uses metaphors with which people can identify. In his first budget message, for example, Reagan described a trillion dollars by comparing it to piling up dollar bills beside the Empire State Building. Reagan, to use one of Alexander Haig's coinages, "tangibilitated" the idea. Leaders make ideas tangible and real to others, so they can support them. For no matter how marvelous the vision, the effective leader must use a metaphor, a word or a model to make that vision clear to others.

In contrast, President Carter was boring. Carter was one of our best-informed presidents; he had more facts at his fingertips than almost any other president. But he never made the meaning come through the facts. I interviewed an assistant secretary of commerce appointed by Carter, who told me that after four years in his administration, she still did not know what Jimmy Carter stood for. She said that working for him was like looking through the wrong side of a tapestry; the scene was blurry and indistinct.

The leader's goal is not mere explanation or clarification but the creation of meaning. My favorite baseball joke is exemplary: In the ninth inning of a key playoff game, with a three-and-two count on the batter, the umpire hesitates a split second in calling the pitch. The batter whirls around angrily and says, "Well, what was it?" The umpire snarls back, "It ain't *nothing* until *I* call it!"

The third competency is management of trust. Trust is essential to all organizations. The main determinant of trust is reliability, what I call *constancy*. When I talked to the board members or staffs of these leaders, I heard certain phrases again and again: "She is all of a piece." "Whether you like it or not, you always know where he is coming from, what he stands for."

When John Paul II visited this country, he gave a press conference. One reporter asked how the pope could account for allocating funds to build a swimming pool at the papal summer palace. He responded quickly, "I like to swim. Next question." He did not rationalize about medical reasons or claim that he got the money from a special source. A recent study showed that people would much rather follow individuals they can count on, even when they disagree with their viewpoint, than people they agree with but who shift positions frequently. I cannot emphasize enough the significance of constancy and focus. Margaret Thatcher's reelection in Great Britain is another excellent example. When she won office in 1979, observers predicted that she quickly would revert to defunct Labor Party policies. She did not. She has not turned; she has been constant, focused, and all of a piece.

The fourth leadership competency is management of self, knowing one's skills and deploying them effectively. Management of self is critical; without it, leaders and managers can do more harm than good. Like incompetent doctors, incompetent managers can make life worse, make people sicker and less vital. There is a term—*iatrogenic*—for illnesses caused by doctors and hospitals. There should be one for illnesses caused by leaders, too. Some give themselves heart attacks and nervous break-downs; still worse, many are "carriers," causing their employees to be ill.

Leaders know themselves; they know their strengths and nurture them. They also have a faculty I think of as the Wallenda Factor. The Flying Wallendas are perhaps the world's greatest family of aerialists and tightrope walkers. I was fascinated when, in the early 1970s, seventy-one-year-old Karl Wallenda said that for him living was walking the tightrope, and everything else was waiting. I was struck with his capacity for concentration on the intention, the task, the decision. I was even more intrigued when, several months later, Wallenda fell to his death while walking a tightrope without a safety net between two high-rise buildings in San Juan, Puerto Rico. Wallenda fell still clutching the balancing pole he had warned his family never to drop lest it hurt somebody below. Later, Wallenda's wife said that before her husband had fallen, for the first time since she had known him he had been concentrating on falling, instead of on walking the tightrope. He had personally supervised the attachment of the guide wires, which he had never done before.

Like Wallenda before his fall, the leaders in my group seemed unacquainted with the concept of failure. What you or I might call a failure, they referred to as a mistake. I began collecting synonyms for the word *failure* mentioned in the interviews, and I found more than twenty: *mistake, error, false start, bloop, flop, loss, miss, foul-up, stumble, botch, bungle . . .* but not *failure.* One CEO told me that if she had a knack for leadership, it was the capacity to make as many mistakes as she could as soon as possible, and thus get them out of the way. Another said that a mistake is simply "another way of doing things." These leaders learn from and use something that doesn't go well; it is not a failure but simply the next step.

Leadership can be felt throughout an organization. It gives pace and energy to the work and empowers the work force. Empowerment is the collective effect of leadership. In organizations with effective leaders, empowerment is most evident in four themes:

- *People feel significant.* Everyone feels that he or she makes a difference to the success of the organization. The difference may be small—prompt delivery of potato chips to a mom-and-pop grocery store or developing a tiny but essential part for an airplane. But where they are empowered, people feel that what they do has meaning and significance.
- *Learning and competence matter.* Leaders value learning and mastery, and so do people who work for leaders. Leaders make it clear that there is no failure, only mistakes that give us feedback and tell us what to do next.
- *People are part of a community.* Where there is leadership, there is a team, a family, a unity. Even people who do not especially like each other feel the sense of community. When Neil Armstrong talks about the Apollo explorations, he describes how a team carried out an almost unimaginably complex set of interdependent tasks. Until there were women astronauts, the men referred to this feeling as "brotherhood." I suggest they rename it "family."
- *Work is exciting.* Where there are leaders, work is stimulating, challenging, fascinating, and fun. An essential ingredient in organizational leadership is pulling rather than pushing people toward a goal. A "pull" style of influence attracts and energizes people to enroll in an exciting vision of the future. It motivates through identification, rather than through rewards and punishments. Leaders articulate and embody the ideals toward which the organization strives.

   People cannot be expected to enroll in just any exciting vision. Some visions and concepts have more staying power and are rooted more deeply in our human needs than others. I believe the lack of two such concepts in modern organizational life is largely responsible for the alienation and lack of meaning so many experience in their work. One of these is the concept of quality. Modern industrial society has been oriented to quantity, providing more goods and services for everyone. Quantity is measured in money; we are a money-oriented society. Quality often is not measured at all but is appreciated intuitively. Our response to quality is a feeling. Feelings of quality are connected intimately with our experience of meaning, beauty, and value in our lives.

Closely linked to the concept of quality is that of dedication to, even love of, our work. This dedication is evoked by quality and is the force that energizes high-performing systems. When we love our work, we need not be managed by hopes of reward or fears of punishment. We can create systems that facilitate our work, rather than being preoccupied with checks and controls of people who want to beat or exploit the system.

Ultimately, in great leaders and the organizations surrounding them, there is a fusion of work and play to the point where, as Robert Frost says, "Love and need are one." How do we get from here to there? I think we must start by studying change.

3

The New Metaphysics
of Our Age

Change is the metaphysics of our age. Everything is in motion now. America has changed from a wilderness to an industrial behemoth to a postindustrial morass, and from an upstart revolutionary to a world power to, in the immortal words of Richard Nixon, "a pitiful giant." America was once a rural society, became an urban society, and is now a suburban society. Even big business has moved to the suburbs, so that people now commute from suburb to suburb, as cities become more and more the province of the very rich and the very poor abiding uneasily together. Government has ranged from small and informal to big and effective to big and dumb, blinded now by its own red tape, functioning more of, by, and for itself than for us.

Our machines have multiplied and subdued us. Our furnaces and automobiles have polluted our air and water. Television has made couch potatoes of us. Fast foods have made us obese. Our children have the bodies of middle-aged people. Computers run our airlines and trains and phones, which may be why none of them run on time or very efficiently. Single-family houses have given way to condos, co-ops, and mobile home parks.

We are capable of virtually destroying the world, but we cannot deal with tiny bands of terrorists. The stock market has never been more volatile. The national deficit is soaring. Cigarette and liquor consumption is down, but marijuana and cocaine consumption is up. The Beatles have been succeeded by the Beastie Boys. What used to be spaghetti and macaroni is now pasta, and our typewriters are now word processors, but we seem to have little to say, and what we do say, we say badly.

Everything mechanical has evolved, become better, more efficient, more sophisticated, while everything organic—from ourselves to tomatoes—has devolved. Like the new tomatoes, we lack flavor and juice and taste. Manufactured goods are far more impressive than the people who make them. We are less good, less efficient, and less sophisticated with each passing decade.

What's going on here? In this century, automobiles have advanced from the Model T to the BMW, Mercedes, and Rolls Royce. In the same period, we have "advanced" from such giants as Teddy Roosevelt, D. W. Griffith, Eugene Debs, Frank Lloyd Wright, Thomas Edison and Albert Michelson to . . . Yuppies.

What's going on is that the people in charge, particularly in business and government, have imposed change rather than inspiring it. We have had far more bosses than leaders, and so, finally, everyone has decided to be his or her own boss. This has led to the primitive, litigious, adversarial society we currently live in. As the mad newscaster in the movie *Network* said, "I'm mad as hell and I'm not going to take it anymore."

What's going on, then, is something unprecedented in human history: a middle-class revolution. The poor in America are so much poorer than they were that they have neither the time nor the energy to revolt. They're just trying to survive in an increasingly hostile world. By the same token, the rich are so much richer than they were, and there are so many more of them than there ever were before, that they literally reside above the fray—in New York penthouses, Concordes, and sublime ignorance of the world below. The middle class aspires to that same sublime ignorance.

A talented and successful dentist told me recently that people now become dentists so that they can make a lot of money fast and go into the restaurant business or real estate, where they will really make money. Young writers and painters are not content to practice their craft and perfect it. Now they want to see and be seen, wheel and deal, and they are as obsessed with the bottom line as are IBM executives. The deal for the publication of a book is far more significant than the book itself, and the cover of *People* magazine is more coveted than a good review in the *New York Times*. The only unions making any noise now are middle-class unions: the American Federation of Teachers and the Hollywood guilds. Professors who once at least professed an interest in teaching are now far more interested in deals—for the book, the TV appearance, the consulting job, the conference in Paris—and leave the teaching to teaching assistants.

In other words, when everyone is his or her own boss, no one is in charge, and chaos takes over. Leaders are needed to restore order, by which I mean not obedience but progress. At the very least, we must begin to use our machines, rather than being used by them. But our least will no longer suffice. It is time for us to control events rather than being controlled by them.

Change occurs in two primary ways: through trust and truth or through dissent and conflict. We have tried dissent and conflict and have not changed but have merely become combative. It's time, then, to try the other route. But we are perpetually angry now, all walking around with chips on our shoulders. In Los Angeles in the early summer of 1987, people suddenly began shooting other people on the freeways. In the summer of 1987, we began sniping at presidential candidates who had already shot themselves down. Our rage seems both mindless and endless.

Positive change requires trust, clarity, and participation. At this juncture, all three seem as distant as Jupiter. But we have reached Jupiter, and so perhaps we can finally reach ourselves. Only people with virtue and vision can lead us out of this bog and back to the high ground.

First, such people must gain our trust. Second, they must express their vision clearly so that we all not only understand but concur. Third, they must persuade us to participate. That seems simple enough, and tidy, but in practice it seldom happens that way. Indeed, any fundamental alteration in the ways we live is apt to be messy and rancorous—especially today, when we are naturally rancorous.

In certain situations, such as in a corporation, change can simply be mandated by the powers that be. But this, of course, leads inevitably to the escalation of rancor. Such was the case at CBS-TV when President Lawrence Tisch decreed budget and staff cuts. Off-air dissent and conflict led to an open-air decline; not only did CBS trail in the ratings, but some of its stars, such as Dan Rather, publicly vented their displeasure.

There are three other avenues of change. Every organization has cliques and cabals. The cliques have the power, the money, and the resources. The cabals, usually younger and always ambitious, have drive and energy. Unless the cliques can co-opt the cabals, revolution is inevitable. This avenue, too, is messy. It can lead to either a stalemate or an ultimate victory for the cabals, if for no other reason than that they have staying power.

Another cause of change is external events, as the forces of society impose themselves on the organization. For example, the auto industry was forced to change its ways and its products, both by government regulation and by foreign competition. Detroit has still not recovered from this tumult. In the same way, student activists forced many universities to virtually rewrite their curricula and add black studies and women's studies programs. Academicians are still debating both the sense and the efficacy of such programs, as they have fundamentally altered not only what students learn but how they learn it.

The final mode of change is more profound. The most significant and influential element in organizational life is what I think of as its culture or paradigm. In *The Structure of Scientific Revolution*, Thomas Kuhn (1970) describes how advances are made in science. He believes that the paradigm in science is akin to a zeitgeist or climate of opinion that governs choices. He defines it as "the constellation of values and beliefs shared by the members of a scientific community that determines the choice, problems which are regarded as significant, and the approaches to be adopted in attempting to solve it." According to Kuhn, the people who have revolutionized science have always been those who have changed the paradigm.

Sociologist Max Weber addressed the same phenomenon when he wrote, "At some time, the color changes. Men become uncertain about the significance of their viewpoints, which they have used unreflectively. The path becomes lost in the dusk. The life of the great problems of culture has passed on. Then science also prepares to change its standpoint and its conceptual apparatus in order to look down from the heights of thought upon the current of events." Weber called the things that govern a profession or group's activities and the ways it deals with dissent "domain assumptions."

Obviously, the people who change not merely the content of a particular discipline but its practice and focus are not only innovators but leaders. Ralph Nader, who refocused the legal profession to address consumer problems, was such a person. Betty Friedan, in truthfully defining how women lived, inspired them to live in different ways. Freud, Keynes, and Gropius, each in his own field, created new metaphors of practice that were both valid and compelling.

It is not the articulation of a profession or organization's goals that creates new practices but rather the imagery that creates the understanding, the compelling moral necessity for the new way. The clarity of the metaphor and the energy and courage its maker brings to it are vital to its acceptance. For example, when Branch Rickey, general manager of the Brooklyn Dodgers, decided to bring black players into professional baseball, he chose Jackie Robinson, a paragon among players and among men.

How do we identify and develop such innovators? How do we spot new information in institutions, organizations, and professions? Innovators, like all creative people, see things differently, think in fresh and original ways. They have useful contacts in other areas, other institutions; they are seldom seen as good organization men or women and often viewed as mischievous troublemakers. The true leader not only is him- or herself an innovator but makes every effort to locate and use other innovators in the organization. He or she creates a climate in which conventional wisdom can be questioned and challenged and one in which errors are embraced rather than shunned in favor of safe, low-risk goals.

Organizations, by definition, are social systems in which people have norms, values, shared beliefs, and paradigms of what is right and what is wrong, what is legitimate and what is not, and how things are done. One gains status and power through agreement, concurrence, and conformity with these paradigms. Therefore, both dissent and innovation are discouraged. Every social system contains these forces for conservatism, for maintaining the status quo at any cost, but it must also contain means for movement, or it will eventually become paralyzed. Basic changes take place very slowly, if at all, because those with the power generally have no knowledge, and those with the knowledge have no power. Anyone with real knowledge of history and the world as it is today could redesign society, develop a new paradigm in an afternoon, but turning theory into fact could take a lifetime—unless the person happened to be president of the United States.

Still, we have to try, because America, too many of its organizations, and most of its citizens are locked into roles and practices that simply do not work. True leaders work to gain the trust of their constituents, communicate their vision lucidly, and thus involve everyone in the processes of change. They then try to use the inevitable dissent and conflict creatively and positively, and out of all that, sometimes, a new paradigm emerges.

A recent Harris poll showed that over 90 percent of the people polled would change their lives dramatically if they could, and in most cases they ranked such intangibles as self-respect, affection, and acceptance higher than status, money, and power. They don't like the way they live now, but they don't know how to change. The poll is additional evidence of our need for real leaders and should serve as impetus and inspiration to potential leaders and innovators. If such people have the will to live up to their potential, and the rest of us have the gumption to follow them, we might finally find our way out of this bog we're in.

PART TWO

A SOCIETY
WITHOUT DREAMS

4

The Long Slide
from True Leadership

Two hundred years ago, when the nation's founders gathered in Philadelphia to write the Constitution, the United States had a population of only 3 million people, yet six world-class leaders contributed to the making of that extraordinary document. Today, there are more than 240 million of us, and we have Ollie North, the thinking man's Rambo. What happened?

As eighteenth-century America was notable for its geniuses, nineteenth-century America for its freewheeling adventurers and entrepreneurs, and early-twentieth-century America for its scientists and inventors, late-twentieth-century America has been notable for its bureaucrats and managers. What those Philadelphia geniuses created and their rowdy successors built, the organization men—in both government and business—have remade, or unmade. Unlike either our nation's founders or the industrial titans, the managers of America's giant corporations and the bureaucrats, elected and appointed, have no gut stake in the enterprise and no vision. More often than not, they're just hired guns, following the money.

In a sense, the practical opportunities and imperatives of

the Industrial Revolution first overshadowed, then overtook, and finally obscured the political and personal opportunities of the American Revolution. Our forebears not only saw the abundance of natural riches but suddenly had the mechanical means to develop them, and, in the rush to do so, they put aside the development of this democracy, along with their own personal development as citizens. The cry was not so much for men to match the mountains as for men to tame mountains and turn them into goods.

The robber barons and adventurers stormed across the land and seized its coal and iron and water and made fortunes for themselves and vital goods and services for everyone else. Those strong, willful, brazen businessmen, explorers, and inventors—not the founding fathers—made and shaped what came to be thought of as American civilization. When the British writer H. G. Wells toured America in the early 1900s, he remarked that our single most impressive achievement was to update the British feudal system and make it efficient.

Not surprisingly, the mass of Americans, who labored in inhuman and inhumane caldrons of factories for little money, ultimately reacted against these high-living, reckless robber barons, and the era of organization men began. This new breed was as cool as their predecessors had been hot, analytical rather than intuitive, and careful rather than careless. More often than not, these hired guns had no vision beyond the quarterly report. It was their job to crank out profits, and that is what they did.

The managers agreed with Calvin Coolidge, who said, "The business of America is business." Their government counterparts, the bureaucrats, saw it differently. They set out to tame the big corporation in the same way that the corporations' founders had tamed the continent itself. The managers parried with lobbyists to tame Congress, and so America continued to bypass democracy in favor of government of, by, and for special interests—that is, capitalism. As bureaucrats and managers traded favors, a kind of stalemate developed. Nothing much grows in a stalemate, of course, but managers and bureaucrats are less gardeners than mechanics, fonder of tinkering with machinery than making things grow.

Having emerged from World War II as the richest and most powerful nation on earth, the United States had lost its edge by the mid-1970s to the two nations it had whipped in the war. The much-bruited American century was suddenly the Japanese century—in business, anyway. It's anyone's guess whose century it has become politically, but tiny, livid Iran certainly seems to have a lock on the 1980s and has made us behave at least as irrationally as it behaves—selling it arms in 1986 only to have those arms turned on us in 1987.

Things do not happen without reasons. We lost the edge because, however skillful managers and bureaucrats are at holding actions, they have no talent at all for advancing. Thus, today, America no longer leads the world and is itself leaderless.

The national rebellion of the 1960s, the "Me Decade" that followed, and today's Yuppies are all consequences of the mistakes and crudities of the organization men. Many of our citizens have come to see the United States as the biggest, most mindless, and clumsiest corporation of all. They can't find either its head or its heart. But, ignoring all the signals, along with their responsibilities, the managers and bureaucrats continue to flex their considerable muscle. White House underlings run covert actions in violation of the law, while corporate honchos gather their wagons in a circle in paranoid preparation for the ultimate shootout. For all their brass, these new business kingpins are not leaders but merely bosses. Like the dinosaurs, though they may tower over their surroundings, they are not necessarily equipped for survival. These bosses confuse quantity with quality and substitute ambition for imagination. Much like Washington's tin soldiers and sunshine patriots, they do not understand the world as it is.

America has been dragged feet first into the late twentieth century. The Soviet Union dictates what passes for our foreign policy, along with our ruinous defense budget. The Japanese and Germans have taken over our primary totems—the automobile and the TV set. Tiny bands of terrorists regularly mug us. Unfriendly dictatorships blackmail us. And we have recently become the world's leading debtor nation. Like the big old American car, America seems too big and too awkward to work very well, much less respond quickly and wisely to events. Like its big corporations, the nation seems devoted to outmoded methods and ideas that were not very good to start with and seems unwilling or unable to change direction, or even to recognize that its foreign and domestic policies are not only outdated but dangerously insufficient.

Our fundamental confusion was perfectly expressed in the presidential election of 1980 when the offspring of the once-radical movements of the 1960s found themselves in step with Ronald Reagan, the man old enough to be their grandfather, the longtime hero of and spokesperson for the far right. With him, they believed that the individual was all, and greed was everything. Self-interest was not only a virtue, it was patriotic.

Once upon a time, we all wanted to be Lindbergh or DiMaggio or Astaire, because they were the best at what they did; now we want to be Pickens, Trump, or Iacocca, because they're rich. Far too often now, our idols are all smoke and mirrors, sound and fury signifying nothing. But they do not rise unassisted. It is our need as much as their greed that catapults them into the spotlight's golden glare.

At the heart of America is a vacuum into which self-anointed saviors have rushed. They pretend to be leaders, and we—half out of envy, half out of longing—pretend to think of them as leaders. Consider that phenomenon Ronald Reagan, the star who became a savior. By 1980, we were thoroughly sick of Jimmy Carter's preaching. Ronnie rode in from the West, full of smiles and assurances, and told us what we had been waiting to hear all our lives: that selfishness was okay. In a cute twist, the oldest president in history made us all feel young and happy again, and never mind that America was running amok abroad and coming unstuck at home.

Our need for true leaders goes unspoken, but it manifests itself in pathetic ways—as in our idolatry of show business stars, our admiration for corporate kings, and our instant elevation of McHeroes such as Ollie North. We didn't much like what he did, but we loved the way that he did it. The recent popularity of instant leadership courses is another symptom of this fundamental need. The courses themselves demonstrate our confusion about what constitutes leadership. Some claim it derives automatically from power. Others say it's mere mechanics—a thorough comprehension of the nature of organizations. Some say that leaders are born, while others argue that they can be made, and according to the one-minute manager and/or microwave theory, made instantly. Pop in Mr. or Ms. Average and out pops another McLeader in sixty seconds.

But billions of dollars are spent annually by and on would-be leaders, yet we have no leaders, and though many corporations now offer leadership courses to their more promising employees, corporate America has lost its lead in the world market. In fact, to this point, more leaders have been made by accident, circumstances, and sheer will than have been made by all the leadership courses.

The Great Depression was the crucible that transformed Franklin D. Roosevelt from politician to leader. Roosevelt's death made Harry Truman president, but sheer will made him a leader. Dwight Eisenhower seemed a likely winner to Republican party bosses, but, once in office, he became his own man, and a leader. Pols such as Chicago's mayor Richard Daley gave John Kennedy a boost into the White House, but he shone there on his own. Like them or not, FDR, Truman, Ike, and JFK were all true leaders, America's last true leaders.

Truman never saw himself as anything but a loser and made no effort to prepare himself to lead the country. Eisenhower was a good soldier blessed with a constellation of better soldiers who ultimately made both his military and political victories possible. Those charming rich boys FDR and JFK were, in the vernacular of the time, traitors to their class but came to be heroes to the people. To an extent, each of these men was his own invention: Truman and Eisenhower, the quintessential small-town boys rising to the top; Roosevelt and Kennedy, driven by ambitious and powerful parents, worldly, but conventional as young men, finally remaking themselves and the world.

True leaders are not born but made, and not made as much by others as by themselves. But that, of course, is not all of it. Lyndon Johnson, Richard Nixon, and Jimmy Carter could reasonably be described as self-made men. Each began poor, each had extraordinary ambition and drive, each seized every opportunity, some legitimate, some illegitimate, and each managed to become president. But each failed to win or engage our hearts, and thus each was driven out of the White House. Elected by a landslide in 1964, Johnson created such havoc that he chose not to run for reelection in 1968. Nixon was forced to resign after the revelations of Watergate, and Carter became one of the few White House incumbents to lose a reelection bid.

All three were highly competent, but their ambitions overrode their talents. Johnson wanted to make a Great Society but made war instead. Nixon wanted less to lead us than to rule us. It was never clear what Carter wanted, besides the White House. In each case, their minds seemed to be closed—to us, and perhaps even to themselves. Whatever vision each may have had went unexpressed. Each was given to saying one thing and doing another, and each seemed to look on his constituents as adversaries. When people questioned the Vietnam War, Johnson questioned their loyalty. Nixon had an "enemies list." And Carter accused us of malingering.

Johnson, Nixon, and Carter were all more driven than driving, and each seemed caught in his own shadows. They were haunted men, shaped far more by their early deprivations than by their later successes. They did not, then, invent themselves but were made, and unmade, by their own histories.

Just as Roosevelt, Truman, and Kennedy made themselves new, and therefore independent and free, Johnson, Nixon, and Carter were used goods, no matter how far they moved from their pinched beginnings, or how high they rose. It is no wonder that, in their wake, we took matters into our own hands. For as surely as Roosevelt, Truman, Eisenhower, and Kennedy invented themselves, and Johnson, Nixon, and Carter were made by their own histories, we invented Ronald Reagan. We made him a star, and then we made him president. It seemed perfect at the time—after all the good guys and all the bad guys, finally a nice guy in the White House. But it hasn't worked out very well. Economically, politically, and socially, America is in far worse shape than it was in 1980—at home and abroad.

No one had been more thoroughly initiated in the rituals of the American Way than Reagan, and no one was better suited to act out those rituals on the quintessential American medium, television. He was the perfect embodiment of The Way. The ancient messages traveled through him into the shining ether without friction. It was as if his believing self were plugged directly into our own wellsprings of belief, activating our desire to believe.

He did not argue for the American Way, he *was* the American Way. He didn't have to persuade us of anything. He merely had to appear. As was once said of *Time* publisher Roy Larson, he didn't have his finger on the national pulse, he was the pulse. Reagan's approach was not didactic, discursive, or sequential. It was associative, strobelike, the all-inclusive montage. We made the necessary connections. He was good-looking, smooth, and selfish, the perfect star for our fantasy, and, like us, he had no higher aspirations, just ambitions. It wasn't his movie, it was ours.

It is said that when Jack Warner (of Warner Brothers) heard that Reagan was running for governor of California, he said, "No, Jimmy Stewart for governor, Ronnie for best friend." As it turns out, Warner was right. Reagan isn't a leader, he's a pal, a buddy, assuming you're upwardly mobile or already there. He was the perfect president for the feel-good 1980s. He said he was okay and we were okay, and greed was okay, and he always smiled, and we thought everything was okay, until we learned about the Iran-Contra scandal. After that, as he put it, he was "beloved, but not believed." We trusted him, and now we don't trust anymore.

The founding fathers and the adventurers and inventors who succeeded them were dreamers, and dreamers on a grand scale. Today, we do not dream but merely fantasize about money and things. As a dreamless sleep is death, a dreamless society is meaningless. As individuals, we need dreams in the way we need air, and as a society, we need true leaders—uncommon men and women who, having invented themselves, can reinvent America and restore the collective dream by expressing for and to us that irreverent, insouciant, peculiarly American spirit.

Right now, there are probably thousands of potential

leaders in America—young men and women full of passion for the promises of life with no outlets for that passion, because we scorn passion even as we reward ambition. If history is to be trusted, they are more likely than not the loners, the kids who seem always to be a little at odds with their peers, off there, looking at life from a different angle—originals, not copies.

Leaders, like anyone else, are the sum of all their experiences, but, unlike others, they amount to more than the sum, because they make more of their experiences. This is the best and worst of all possible worlds for bright young would-be leaders: best because their opportunities for personal achievement are unlimited, worst because America has never been less interested in achievement or more interested in success. Everyone insists on having his or her own way now—from Reagan, who sees Congress less as a coequal branch of government than as an obstacle, to the young Yuppie who shoves in at the head of the movie line.

The conflicts between individual rights and the common good are far older than the nation, but they have never been as sharp or as mean as they are today. In fact, as the upwardly mobile person has replaced the citizen, we have less and less in common and less and less that is good. The founding fathers based the Constitution on the assumption that there was such a thing as public virtue. James Madison wrote, "The public good . . . the real welfare of the great body of people . . . is the supreme object to be pursued." At the moment, we not only cannot agree on what the public good is, we show no inclination to pursue it.

The notion of public virtue was replaced early on by special interests that were succeeded, in the 1960s, by what we call, vaguely, "values." Robert N. Bellah and his coauthors define values in *Habits of the Heart* as "the incomprehensible, indefensible thing that the individual chooses when he or she has thrown off the last vestige of external influence and reached pure contentless freedom." The promised Great Society of the 1960s has evolved into what Bellah and his coauthors (1985) call "a permissive therapeutic culture . . . which urges a strenuous effort to make our particular segment of life a small world of its own."

People are literally retreating into their electronic castles, working at home and communicating with the world via computers; screening their calls on answering machines, ordering in movies for their VCRs, food for their microwave ovens, and trainers for their bodies; and keeping the world at bay with advanced security systems. Trend spotters call this phenomenon "cocooning," but it might more accurately be described as terminal egocentricity.

As a nation cannot survive without virtue, it cannot progress without some common vision, and we haven't had a real sense of purpose, as a people, since the 1960s. A healthy, productive society is based in high expectations. The individual expects society to be virtuous, just, and productive. As the individual must continually challenge society to live up to its promises, society, at the same time, must continually encourage the individual to fulfill his or her promise. At the moment, neither the individual nor society seems interested in doing better—except on the most atavistic level. It abuses us, and we use it.

But since we are the society, we can't expect it to do better until we do better, and we will not do better until we emerge from our cocoons. We show no inclination to do that, and there is on the horizon no leader who seems capable of inspiring or moving us in a more positive direction. For those who would argue that there is Jesse Jackson, who can certainly rouse people with his vision of things as they could and should be, I must respond that he is, like Ronald Reagan, a creation of our times, one who has shown consummate understanding of both media and public, but Jackson has shown little or no steadiness, so that both his judgment and his character are called into question. Jackson preaches a better game than he practices.

No, for the moment, anyway, we don't seem to want leaders. In these mean, greedy times, we seem to prefer co-conspirators, and that is exactly what we have—in the White House, the boardrooms, even the classrooms. There is, then, no doubt that we could do better but considerable doubt as to whether we want to, and so we are destined to drift on dreamlessly, secure in our cocoons of self-interest.

5

Back to the Future

In America, the 1960s were and still are the future, because we never really got there. We talked a good game and fought the good fight, and we dreamed of the perfect society, but it remained a dream. In an address to the American Psychological Association in Los Angeles (September 1964), I imagined

> A new concept of man, based on increased knowledge of his complex and shifting needs, which replaces an over-simplified, innocent push-button idea of man, a new concept of power, based on collaboration and reason, which replaces a model of power based on coercion and threat, a new concept of organizational values, based on democratic ideals, which replaces the depersonalized mechanistic value system of democracy. The social structure of organizations of the future will have some unique characteristics. The key word will be temporary. There will be adaptive rapidly changing temporary systems. Groups will be arranged on an organic rather than mechanical model. They will evolve in response to a problem rather than to programmed

role expectations. People will be evaluated not vertically according to rank and status, but flexibly and functionally, according to skill and professional training. Adaptive problem-solving, temporary systems of diverse specialists, linked together by coordinating and task-evaluating executive specialists in an organic flux—this is the organization form that will gradually replace bureaucracy as we know it.

I not only declared bureaucracy dead, I said that democracy was finally inevitable. We were going to revolutionize organizations in the same way that Yippies and hippies, college students, and minorities were going to revolutionize society. We were finally going to make America work by redesigning the way it worked. The Yippies and hippies made a few gains before they grew up and went to Wall Street or became major drug dealers, or both. Minorities and women gained some token ground, much of which they have since lost, but bureaucracy did not die, and, with some notable exceptions, organizations did not change. As it turned out, America went right by democracy and on to anarchy. We gave a free-for-all and everyone came, and it was everyone for him- or herself.

It was the dawn of the age of what was originally called the Human Potential Movement, when we listened as Abraham Maslow and Carl Rogers beckoned, when everyone wanted to become self-actualized, whatever that meant. We went to seminars and workshops and encounter groups, we got our heads together and knew where we were coming from. But we were blissfully unaware of where we were going, and so the decade became home to the "Me Generation."

What we saw as a breakthrough turned out to be a breakdown. We thought that the rigid hierarchical system in which everyone has his or her place, the traditional bureaucratic pyramid with the boss up there riding point and the rest of us bowing obediently, was not only counterproductive but obsolete. After all, if kids could be free, so could the rest of us, and free people are productive people are happy people. New trees sprouted in the groves of academe: organization development, human resources development, out of which came perfect systems, in which people could not only function efficiently but flourish. We declared that these new systems were means, not ends. We opened all the windows, figuratively speaking, of course, since office windows haven't actually opened for a generation. We threw out institutional colors and furniture and brought in macrame and hanging plants and paintings and sculptures. We lobbied for and got maternity leaves, sensitivity training, and retreats, and we were sympathetic to midlife crises, which we, not incidentally, invented. We developed new values, too.

In 1969, I summarized these values in *The Temporary Society* (Chapter Three): "Full and free communication, regardless of rank and power; a reliance on consensus rather than the more customary forms of coercion or compromise to manage conflict; the idea that influence is based on technical competence and knowledge rather than on the vagaries of personal whims or the prerogatives of power; an atmosphere that permits and even encourages emotional expression as well as task-oriented acts; a basically human bias, one that accepts the inevitability of conflict between the organization and the individual, but that is willing to cope with and mediate this conflict on rational grounds."

I also wrote there, "We must eternally confront and test our humanness and strive to become more fully human. We operate on a narrow range of the full spectrum of human potential, and, for the most part, our organizational lives tend to compress the possibilities even more. . . . To be fully human means that we must work hard at coming to terms with unfamiliar aspects of our personalities and it means we have to work equally hard to get other people to widen their responses so that they can understand and accept unfamiliarity and uncertainty. It also means that we must be able to absorb our common humanness without fear of absorption or nothingness."

It was an extraordinary time in the life of this republic. We were on the verge not only of finally achieving what our forebears had only imagined but of taking a giant step forward in human evolution. We were ready to become . . . heroic, meaning fully human, meaning courageous, meaning complete, meaning sympathetic, in the most profound sense, to the aspirations and needs of our fellow human beings. We were, in a word, nuts.

We thought we could do what Buddha, Jesus, Lincoln, and Franklin Roosevelt couldn't do. We thought we could not simply change human nature but improve it. In its life, America has four times come face to face with its amazing aspirations. The first time, we traded the American Revolution for the Industrial Revolution, believing that we could wait to be fully human and free but we could not wait to be rich. The second time, the good guys won the Civil War, but the bad guys kept control of the machinery. The third time, in one of history's more impressive ironies, World War II halted our first authentic effort to achieve something like the democracy our founders had imagined. It is less cynical than honest to say that we welcomed the interruption. The fourth time—the 1960s—everything was in motion again, everything but human nature. We emerged from that tumultuous decade sadder, no wiser, but liberated—free to be me and me, *never* us.

In the mid-1960s, we protested abuses and misuses of authority on such gut issues as civil rights and Vietnam. By 1970, we were denying the legitimacy of all traditional authority, and by the mid-1970s, we were declaring that each of us was his or her own authority. In the 1960s, we said that salvation resided in better systems, systems based on consensus rather than authority; by the 1970s, we had decided that salvation depended on better people, but by better we meant freer, and when everybody is determined to be free, free to be I and me, consensus is hard to come by. We did not see that we couldn't have it both ways, couldn't have both consensus and absolute freedom. It was a fool's game, and so everyone won and we all lost.

The primary lesson of the Human Potential Movement was that we have far more potential for antisocial behavior than anyone had heretofore imagined. Our notions of freedom and democracy were made manifest as license and anarchy. People weren't interested in ideas and philosophy. They wanted recipes, quick fixes, formulas. Our gurus Maslow and Rogers told us we

could create our own reality, and we did. But damned if we
didn't put off being fully human again, and go for the gold.
Again.

Where did we go wrong? America has always been at war
with itself. We have always dreamt of community and democracy but always practiced individualism and capitalism. We have
celebrated innocence but sought power. We are the world's leading sentimentalists, and it's a very short step from sentimental-
ity to cynicism. Indeed, the sentimentalist—whether charming
like Cole Porter or monstrous like Adolph Hitler—inevitably becomes a cynic, and so it has been with America the Sentimental.

In the '50s, America suffered an unprecedented failure of
nerve. We had won World War II and ruled the world. Every
other nation was physically and spiritually devastated, but we
were relatively unscathed, and richer and more powerful than
we had ever been before. Then, suddenly, we were convinced
that the Russians were about to pounce on us, and so, in some
strange frenzy, we began inflicting wounds on ourselves. All of
the Soviet Union's legions could not have dented our national
spirit and meaning more than McCarthyism did.

The 1960 presidential election was a kind of referendum
on insiders versus outsiders. Nixon was the pluperfect insider,
the boss, and John Kennedy was the pluperfect outsider, the
young challenger. Kennedy's victory seemed to signal the beginning of a new era. But then he, his brother Bobby, and Martin
Luther King were murdered, and the bosses took over again.

Joseph Conrad said in a letter to H. G. Wells, "The difference between us, Wells, is fundamental. You don't care for humanity, but think they are to be improved. I love humanity, but
know they are not." In my line of work, I've been required to
believe that people can and will improve—with a little encour-
agement. In the last twenty years, I've seen that people either
can't be improved or don't want to be improved.

Which brings me to the three horsemen of the modern
apocalypse: Marx, Darwin, and Freud, who turned their questions into answers and thus raised fundamental questions, which
we have failed to address. They were determinists, the designers
of the modern world. Marx said, "It is not the consciousness of

men that determines their existence, but on the contrary it is their social existence which determines their consciousness." Freud said, "The rider is obliged to guide his horse in the direction in which it itself wants to go." Darwin wrote, "I have called this principle . . . natural selection . . . the expression often used by Mr. Herbert Spencer, of the survival of the fittest, is more accurate."

According to the three horsemen, then, our circumstances, present and past, conscious and unconscious, genetic and learned, make monkeys of us all. But, led by Maslow and Rogers, we absorbed everything the determinists had to teach us and became relativists anyway, vowing to change our circumstances and thereby to change ourselves and our fate. What we failed to see, or failed to admit, anyway, was that in making our circumstances more encouraging, generous, and open, we were not tempering fate so much as tempting it.

Freud decreed that each of us was three: the id, the ego, and the superego, or ambition, competence, and conscience. In this brave new world, this age of ambition, id is it. Our ambitions have killed off our conscience and made competence irrelevant. If competence counted for anything now, would Prince be king, and would Sylvester Stallone, alias Rambo, get $12 million per extended grunt? In loosening our social bonds, we cut ourselves loose, and we're adrift, victims of our own hubris. That's the bad news.

A random list of words beginning with the letter C: *can, commune, community, citizen, civic, corporate, container, colony, circle, concern, create, collage, compassion, comedian, commitment.* A random list of words beginning with the letter I: *integrity, independence, isolation, ideology, idiographic, island, idiosyncratic, ignorance, inspiration, idiot, id.* Are we meant to be islands or circles? Is inspiration more useful than commitment? Are idiots actually comedians? Is it an accident that C is nearly a circle, while I is a stick? Is it pure chance that so many words signifying separateness start with I, while so many words that start with C signify groups? Truth begins with questions. Order emerges from chaos. That's the good news.

Conrad was right. Humanity cannot be improved. That's

good news, too. It was never our job to make a new race, but it
was and is our job to do the best we can with what we have on
hand. Ambition got us into this fix. Competence and conscience
will get us out. We don't have all the answers. We don't even
know what the questions are.

Alfred North Whitehead wrote, "In this modern world,
the celibacy of the medieval learned class has been replaced by a
celibacy of the intellect which is divorced from the concrete
contemplation of the complete facts." And he didn't even know
about Wall Street insiders, the Iran-Contra scandal, or Gary Hart.

Ivan Boesky, Ollie North, and Gary Hart have, at the very
least, celibacy of the intellect in common. They, along with
their less infamous counterparts all over America, are so egocen-
tric, so absorbed in their own adventures that they see the rest
of the world as an encumbrance, an annoyance. If the world had
not got in the way, Boesky would still be running deals, North
would still be running guns, and Hart would still be running for
president. As Hart's farewell address so vividly demonstrated,
the flaw was not in him but in the system. This sort of intellectual celibacy is bound to turn into profligacy, which ruins the
celibate and damages the system. To know everything about
one thing is to understand nothing about anything. Had Hart,
Boesky, or North engaged in concrete contemplation of the
facts, they might have saved themselves, and the rest of us,
from their profligate actions.

Hart, Boesky, and North are not exceptions, they are the
rule now in this wilderness we have made for ourselves. The
physical world is elegant in design, predictable in action, and
fixed in purpose. The social world, the world we have made, is
vastly inelegant, unpredictable, and unfixed. Made of ambiguity
and ambivalence, contradiction and conflict, it is a clown in the
temple. It can change as you look at it. Sometimes, it changes
because you are looking at it. It requires alertness, curiosity, im-
patience, courage, and skepticism—qualities that are in very
short supply in everyone over twenty-one, but proliferating in
the very young.

Our children know more than we do now, and what they
know has made them premature cynics. They may be woefully

ignorant of history, philosophy, and literature, since what passes for public education in this country has deteriorated into a nationwide system of holding pens, but they are street-smart—alert, curious, impatient, brave, and exceedingly skeptical. They are also sad and mad. The incidence of teenage suicide, drug addiction, and pregnancies has reached epidemic proportions. Teens communicate almost exclusively in four-letter words, filling the gaps with "like" and "you know." We have taught them so badly that they cannot express their rage coherently and so must demonstrate it. They are simultaneously post- and preliterate, far more comfortable with images than with words, given, like their principal heroes, to "acting out." They say to each other and to us, "get real," but, having created our own reality, which is anything but real, we don't know where to begin.

6

The Age of Unreality

If America has any point at all now, and I am by no means convinced that it does, it is to avoid reality. It is as if the entire nation had decided to stop facing facts. As he abruptly left the
1988 presidential race, Gary Hart suggested, quite sincerely,
that he was too good for us. Defrocked minister Jim Bakker insisted that he had had an affair with secretary Jessica Hahn in
order to save his marriage. Hahn countered by saying that it
wasn't an affair, it was rape, took more than $200,000 to keep
silent, and then not only talked but did a *Playboy* interview and
posed for the usual *Playboy* centerfold shots. This, she said,
proved not only that was she a free person but that God was on
her side. Ronald Reagan, having said initially that he knew
nothing about the gun runs to the Nicaraguan Contras, later said
that not only had he known about it, but it had been his idea.

In the same vein, Ollie North's secretary, Fawn Hall, declared, by way of justifying breaking the law, that sometimes
you have to obey "a higher law." And North himself admitted
that he had not only lied but destroyed evidence—but told Congress that he was telling it the truth. Presidential candidate Joe
Biden not only lied about his academic achievements and borrowed passages from other people without crediting them, he

borrowed the life of an English politician, claiming that he was the first Biden in "a thousand generations" to go to college.

Meanwhile, Wall Street traders became victims of their own practical jokes, TV minister Oral Roberts went up in a tower and said that God would strike him dead if people didn't immediately send him lots of money, and TV minister turned presidential candidate Pat Robertson went to Bedford-Stuyvesant, one of New York's most ravaged sections, to announce his candidacy, because he had once briefly been a minister there. This was news to area residents, who protested his presence as, at the very least, exploitative. Football great Rosey Grier, who once served Bobby Kennedy and after Kennedy's assassination drifted steadily to the right politically, sort of summed up our general confusion by introducing Robertson and his wife as "Mr. and Mrs. Robinson."

Rather than protesting all this doubletalk, the American people seem not only to accept it but to understand it. This, then, is the Age of Unreality.

Of course, reality has never been our strong suit. "Oh, beautiful for spacious skies, for amber waves of grain, for purple mountains' majesty above the fruited plain. . . ." By 1893, when Katherine Lee Bates wrote "America the Beautiful," once-pastoral America had become a vast blast furnace, and more Americans sang about spacious skies, amber waves of grain, and fruited plains than ever saw them, but never mind. They were out there somewhere, and, if we got rich enough or brave enough, we could go and see them for ourselves.

But if we were vague and dreamy in 1893, today we are only semiconscious, real people living in an imaginary landscape. In Thoreau's phrase, we have become the tools of our tools. We invented a whole range of amazing machines, and now they are reinventing us. Ironically, the more sophisticated they become, the more primitive we become, and the more active they are, the more passive we are. And the real world has receded and receded.

The majority of us now live in cities and suburbs, vast, shapeless megamixes of shopping centers, fast-food parlors, supermarkets, freeways, and the occasional lawn, which by now may be astroturf. But this is all merely a backdrop, the setting for the action. And there's plenty of action—advertising, radio, TV, movies, rock 'n' roll, fashion, evangelism, and journalism, a twenty-four-hours-a-day, seven-days-a-week, fifty-two-weeks-a-year whirlwind of sound, images, ideas, faces. Everything is in motion, but nothing is happening. We have become extras in this perpetual national drama. At parties, people talk about whoever is in the headlines at the moment. The hostess at a recent dinner party explained that several invited guests had called to cancel. They were staying home to watch the season finale of the television show "Dallas." She seemed to think it was perfectly reasonable that these highly sophisticated, educated people (who presumably had VCRs) had opted to spend the evening with the Ewings rather than with friends.

But, of course, the Ewings—J. R., Bobby, Miss Ellie, Pam, and the rest—*are* friends, and television is not just entertainment, it's life. It's bigger than all of us, and it's miraculous. It can bring the entire world into our bedroom. It's there, busy, pumping away all day, all night, every day, every night. It never sleeps. You wake up at three in the morning, turn on the TV, and there's Charley Rose talking to Alexander Haig. Of course, it isn't really three in the morning where they are. It's six in the morning, but they probably taped the interview at four o'clock the afternoon of the previous day. They're in Washington. We know that, because an announcer tells us so. Sometimes, you can see the Washington Monument over Charley's shoulder. But maybe it isn't the monument, maybe it's a giant photo.

So here we are, at three in the morning, in Los Angeles, watching two men who say they're in Washington, where it's 6 A.M., only they're probably in bed, maybe in Washington, maybe someplace else, because we're really watching a tape. Maybe. It should be confusing, but it isn't, because we're very advanced. We understand this stuff. We understand that the TV, the box, the instrument, the appliance, is our world now, our landscape, our context. Everything that really matters happens on the box. Gary Hart withdraws, Jim Bakker confesses, Oral Roberts commands, Pam Ewing dies (maybe), the Carringtons are kidnapped. And, for God's sake, there's a fire in Hill Street.

"Hill Street Blues" is over, of course. Not because of the fire, but because people got bored and the ratings declined. Actually, it's not really over. It'll be around in reruns until the year 2000. That's one of the amazing things about the box. It can contain *everything,* everything that matters, anyway, no matter how much everything there is. The box's capacity is infinite. Ads, rock 'n' roll, wars, peace, cities, people, moments, murders, dancers, everything is in the box. It forgets nothing. Dial around enough, you'll even find spacious skies, amber waves of grain, and fruited plains in there. The new context, then, is no context, is everything and nothing, fact and fiction, history and right now.

And here's the amazing thing: everything is equal. The assassination of John Kennedy and David Letterman's stupid dog tricks are absolutely equal. TV is the ultimate democracy, the great leveler. In this new context of no context, which *New Yorker* writer George W. S. Trow first identified in 1978, everything has the same weight, and nothing is ever over. Jim Bakker, "Wheel of Fortune," and "Miami Vice" get not merely equal but precisely the same treatment.

Everything is in living color (which is an oxymoron, but in the Age of Unreality, everything is an oxymoron), and in two dimensions, but without size (on my set, Ted Koppel's head is about two inches high; on your larger set, it may be life-size, but neither of us can see his feet). We see parts of everything—people, places, and things. We have no sense of space or distance, because TV can go from Nashville to New York to your bedroom in a wink. That's comforting, of course. We're all just one big happy family. Here I am, in my bedroom, and here the entire world is, in my bedroom, too, and I know Letterman and Johnny Carson better than I know my neighbors. Carson has told us all about his divorces. I have no idea whether any of my neighbors have ever been divorced, or whether they're married to the people they're living with now, or whether, indeed, they're living with anyone. There is a kind of intimacy about TV—actors and musicians talking about drug problems, marital difficulties, deals gone bad, "sharing" everything. I don't mind. They get it off their chests, but I don't have to do anything about it. I don't even have to worry about it, and I can talk about it at parties, because it's not a secret. There are no secrets now.

This, then, is the best sort of intimacy. We know everything, but we don't have to do anything. Gary Hart doesn't want to say whether he has committed adultery or not, but he's the exception here. Almost everyone else—from Shelley Winters to Jimmy Swaggart—has already confessed.

In ABC Sports' immortal phrase, everything "is up close and personal," but it is, of course, also very far away. Surely, in the Age of Unreality, this is the best of all possible arrangements. We're in on everything, but unscathed by it, untouched; involved but not responsible.

TV is the dominant medium. Everything else looks more and more like TV. *Us* and *People* magazines are print versions. David Salle's paintings are paint versions. Top-forty radio stations are audio versions. Some clothing stores now use closed-circuit TV to show you the clothes that are on the racks. More people look at the clothes on TV than on the racks. In the same way, audiences at tapings of TV shows are more comfortable watching the TV monitors than watching the actual actors on actual sets. No wonder. TV has shown itself to be far more trustworthy than the real world. Husbands, wives, friends, presidents come and go, but TV is always there. We move; it moves along with us. TV prefers movement and pictures to stillness and words. Now we all do. While we enjoy hearing rock stars or all the legions of unhappy, even warped people who pass by Donahue's cameras telling their secrets to us, we don't much enjoy people talking about issues, people just sitting there, looking at us, discussing foreign policy or religion or literature. From TV, we have learned to handle images, avalanches of them, blizzards of them, but ideas are so, well, dull. If you can't see them, how can you understand them?

When Ronald Reagan talks to us on TV, we understand everything, but when he talks to us on the radio, when we can hear him but not see him, we don't understand. He sounds old, raspy, cranky, like the old man in the hardware store who's always mad about something. It was just the opposite with Richard

Nixon. He used to sound pretty reasonable on the radio, but when we saw him, he seemed quite mad. We incline toward attractive people, pretty images. Ideas are often neither attractive nor pretty, and they're demanding, they require us to work. The new content then is no content. Just show us everything; we'll think about it later.

Given our belief in image, the ascension of actor Ronald Reagan to the White House not only was fitting, it was inevitable. You want a leader who understands what's going on, and what's going on is TV. So what if he didn't know much about politics. He knew all about TV, knew the value of a wink and a smile, knew how to look right through the camera into our hearts. He was perfect, until the Iran-Contra scandal. Suddenly, he began trying to explain things, and we hate it when that happens. Now he's like the guest who overstays his welcome. We want him to go home.

The Democrats haven't been able to get our attention because there hasn't been a Democrat since John Kennedy who really understood the new context and was comfortable in it. It's as if they have a death wish. Lyndon Johnson, Hubert Humphrey, George McGovern, Jimmy Carter, and Walter Mondale all had awful, grating voices; none but McGovern was good-looking, and he was balding. These were not men you wanted in your house on anything like a regular basis. Gary Hart wasn't bad-looking, and he has plenty of hair and a nice speaking voice, calm, deep, unshrill, but then he began to behave like J. R. Ewing. Now, we love J. R., but we wouldn't choose him to be president.

As for Michael Dukakis, the nicest thing that was said about him was that if George Bush reminded every woman of her first husband, Michael Dukakis reminded every woman of her second. He seemed to possess ample character and judgment, but all told, he was more of an effective manager than a bold leader. If the Democrats had any sense at all, they would draft a real TV veteran—Jim Garner, for instance. He's good-looking, we all know him and like him, and he's mastered TV, handles it as well as or better than anyone else. We're a whole lot more comfortable with stars than with leaders. Leaders not only are unreliable, they're demanding. John Kennedy said, "Ask not what your country can do for you—ask what you can do for your country." Stars are entertaining and undemanding. Even when they fall from grace, and end up at the Betty Ford Center, they're entertaining. We love confessions, ours and other people's, the franker the better now, and the line between stars' lives and roles is virtually invisible. "Moonlighting" star Bruce Willis is a scamp on and off the box, as his scuffle with Los Angeles cops proved. Jimmy Smits of "L.A. Law" is now in trouble with the law. Maybe Smits the TV lawyer will end up winning an acquittal for Smits the citizen. There's a kind of wonderful symmetry about all this. Elizabeth Taylor portrays alcoholics and becomes an alcoholic herself. She marries Richard Burton on screen and off. She marries and divorces other men, off and on screen, until finally it all sort of melts together, and we can't separate real life from reel life.

In addition to being attractive, interesting, rich, and entertaining, stars know all the stories we like, and we do like stories; some, in fact, we love. As described by Robert Reich (1987) in *Tales of a New America*, there are four we especially like: "The Mob at the Gates," "The Triumphant Individual," "The Benevolent Community," and "The Rot at the Top." We live by them, and TV lives on them. These are not merely our central morality tales, the core of American mythology; they are the bases for virtually all of our TV and film diversions—the basic plots. TV and film don't merely imitate life now, they are life.

In "The Mob at the Gates," it's America versus foreigners and foreign influences. The Russians, the Cubans, the Iranians, the Nicaraguans, the Japanese, the Germans are all out there, waiting to pounce on us. But we are alert, courageous, and proud and will not succumb—not as long as we have Charlton Heston and Clint Eastwood and Sylvester Stallone and Chuck Norris out there defending us.

In "The Triumphant Individual," the little guy wins—again and again, by himself, unassisted, powered by grit and guts. Goldie Hawn beats the system in Washington, Eddie Murphy wins in Philadelphia and Beverly Hills, Steve Martin gets the girl, even if he has a grotesque nose. We can win, too, any time we want to. That's one of the glories of America.

Another glory is demonstrated in "The Benevolent Community," the good-neighbor syndrome. When someone's in trouble, we rally around, pitch right in, and help out. We're the most generous, the kindest people on earth. Everyone knows that.

There are villains, of course. There are always villains. They, of course, are "The Rot at the Top," the big businessmen, such as Burl Ives and Ned Beatty, the political bosses, such as Broderick Crawford, and the Mafia dons, such as De Niro and Pacino and Brando. They have their ways with us—but, of course, we're on to them, so they never get very far. TV and movies tell us these stories so often and so well and blend fact and fiction so smoothly that we believe this is it: America in the box, in our heads. It's all we know and all we need to know.

Octavio Paz (1962) wrote, in *Labyrinth of Solitude*, "Would it be more accurate to say that the North American wants to use reality rather than to know it?" Yes. We have used it, and we do not merely use it but manhandle it now. TV, in particular, has permitted us to do what we have always wanted to do: rewrite, rearrange, reshape, and box reality to suit us. In the Age of Unreality, all of the people fool themselves all of the time.

The question is, then, who did it? Have we done it to ourselves? Was it done to us? Or did it just happen? Social critics are divided. The more cynical say we did it to ourselves, that we are a childlike species with a low tolerance level for reality. We can take only so much at a time, and virtually none now. Less cynical critics say it was done to us, that media moguls have conspired to hypnotize the nation. Why would they do that? To sell us things, say the critics.

I think they're all wrong. I think it just happened. We've always been mechanical wizards, perhaps because America is far more a product of the Industrial Revolution than the American Revolution, and so we just kept inventing machines to improve our lives, and we have improved ourselves right into this pleasant oblivion. Since we aren't fond of reality anyway, we were particularly susceptible to our own sleight of hand, so it's worked out nicely. Now that we're here, we're quite happy. Life is easy, entertaining, and undemanding. Isn't that what we always wanted—the good life? I think so.

Technologically, we're very advanced. We've always had a gift for thinking of and then making highly sophisticated machines. Psychologically, however, we're babes in the woods. We don't understand ourselves or anyone else very well. So, again and again, we've made machines that, in turn, have remade us. This makes social critics crazy, but it doesn't seem to bother us at all.

7

Where Have All
the Leaders Gone?

Roosevelt, who challenged a nation to overcome its fear; Winston Churchill, who demanded and got blood, sweat, and tears from his people; Albert Schweitzer, who from the jungles of Lambaréné inspired a reverence for life; Albert Einstein, who gave us a sense of unity in infinity; Gandhi, David Ben-Gurion, Golda Meir, and Anwar Sadat, who rallied their people to great and humane causes; Jack and Bobby Kennedy and Martin Luther King, Jr., who said we could do better—all are gone now. Where are their successors? Why have we not had any true leaders in the White House in a generation? Why are there no potential presidents who inspire or even excite us? Where, for God's sake, have all the leaders gone?

In the last two decades, there has been a high turnover, an appalling mortality—both occupational and actuarial—among leaders. In the last several decades, the shelf life of college presidents and CEOs has been markedly reduced. In the 1950s, the average tenure for college presidents was over eleven years; today, it's more like four years. In the same way, corporate chieftains' days at the top seem to be numbered from the moment they take office.

In previous generations, at any given moment, there were a half dozen university heads who were known and respected throughout the world. James Conant, Robert Hutchins, Clark Kerr, and their like did not merely run their universities but led a kind of constant national colloquy on the state of education in America. Their turf was not simply their university but all of education, and so when they saw flaws in secondary schools, they not only pointed them out but offered solutions. I cannot remember the last time any university president addressed any problems beyond his or her own campus. Universities have changed, and so have university presidents.

In business, the landscape is equally flat. The great leaders who come to mind—Ford, Edison, Rockefeller, Morgan, Schwab, Sloan, Kettering—are long gone. Reagan's business chums are entrepreneurs outside the business establishment, such as Justin Dart, the drugstore cowboy. Other corporate heads are either organization men who've risen to the level of their incompetence, such as GM's Roger Smith; celebrities, such as Lee Iacocca; or one-man bands, such as Ted Turner, T. Boone Pickens, and Donald Trump, who devote at least as much time and energy to blowing their own horns as to business. It is not an accident that the most celebrated businessmen now are those who spend their days demolishing rather than creating companies.

Things are no different in politics or public service. In 1987, more distinguished people announced that they would not seek the presidency than announced that they would. Gary Hart's and Joe Biden's campaigns collapsed almost before they started. Hollow men in a hollow era.

The problem isn't just ours. It's worldwide. No country—from here to Great Britain to Germany to Israel and Egypt—has the kind of leadership it once had and now needs more urgently than ever. It's as if humanity, to paraphrase Teilhard de Chardin, is falling suddenly out of control of its own destiny. The primary cause is easy to state but nearly impossible to do anything about.

Humanity's principal enemy is human beings. Never before have individuals wanted and been able to seize so much power unto themselves, and never before have they had so many tools to ensure their autonomy. The automobile, the TV, the VCR, the microwave oven, the computer all serve not only to separate us from our fellow humans but to render us independent of them. But it is the anarchic instinct that has blossomed in so many of us, not the tools, that are at the heart of the problem.

This, of course, raises the old chicken-and-egg question. Which came first, a decline in able leaders or a rise in the anarchic instinct? The notion of the public good, the common accord has always been at odds with traditional American individualism, but it blew apart in the explosive 1960s, when virtually every institution came under fire. It is not a coincidence, I think, that in the '60s we also lost three leaders to assassins. John and Robert Kennedy and Martin Luther King were, like them or not, this country's last true national leaders. None of John Kennedy's successors in the White House has enjoyed the consensus he built, and every one of them ran into trouble, of his own making, while in office. In the same way, none of this country's national spokespeople since Robert Kennedy and Dr. King has had the attention and respect they enjoyed. It is as if the nation suffered a nervous breakdown in the 1960s and hasn't even begun to recover.

We lost our leaders, found no one to replace them, and decided to do it ourselves. We questioned everyone in authority and every institution. We formed blocs of like-minded people to agitate for what we wanted and oppose what we didn't want. We went into the streets and onto the barricades. In this light, Lee Harvey Oswald, James Earl Ray, and Sirhan Sirhan can be said to be the principal architects of contemporary America.

Bereft of leaders and bereaved, we turned on the managers and bureaucrats, the organization men who had reduced great private corporations to money mills and great public institutions to red tape. They had not made life easy for us, and now we were going to make life difficult for them.

As individual autonomy waxed, institutional autonomy waned. External forces impinged and imposed more and more on the perimeter of our institutions; the incessant concatenation of often contrary demands grew. The government had for decades assumed more and more power over corporations and institutions. Now the people were challenging not only the government but the corporations and institutions, too. An incessant, dissonant clamor grew.

It was a new kind of populism, not the barn burners of the Grange days, not the "free silver" of Bryanism, but the fragmentation, the caucusization of constituencies. This fragmentation, which existed in virtually every organization, marked the end not only of community, a sense of shared values and symbols, but of consensus. There was Lyndon Johnson pleading, "Come let us reason together," at a time when all these factions scarcely wanted to be together. As Abbie Hoffman said when accused of conspiracy, "Are you kidding? We couldn't agree on lunch."

Everyone went his or her own way. No one wanted to be part of mainstream America; everyone wanted instead to be black or Chicano or a woman or a gay or a Native American. The very idea of the much-heralded "melting pot" or even a milder assimilation was suspect.

A new form of politics was invented—King Caucus, who has more heads than Cerberus, and contending Queens who cry "Off with their heads," as they play croquet with flamingos. It was the politics of multiple advocacies—vocal, demanding, deliberately out of sync, made up of people who were fed up with being ignored, neglected, excluded, denied, subordinated. In the 1960s, they marched. In the 1970s, they sued. The law had suddenly become the court of first resort. America became an increasingly litigious society. In the first litigious flush, an injured hockey player sued his team owner, a student at the University of Bridgeport sued to recover her $150 tuition because she "didn't learn anything," and, in perhaps the most piquant instance, a law review was sued for rejecting an article.

Our new reliance on the courts has not only diminished the autonomy of institutions, it has threatened the autonomy of the individual. Consider the plight of surgeons. If they simply trust their own judgment and do what they believe is best for their patients, they may find themselves facing a court judgment, and so they are less likely to do what they think is medically right than to do what they think is legally safe.

We use the law now as a weapon rather than a tool. It is less and less the basis for our common accord and more and more a primary source of our continuing discord. The confusion, ambiguity, and complexity of the law—augmented by conflicting judicial interpretations—tend toward paralysis. Worse, court judgments have begun to replace expertise as the ultimate measure.

In this new anarchic state, Americans see the law less as an instrument of protection than as an instrument of assault. We are less interested in preserving our common rights than in exercising our individual rights, and *versus* is now the preposition of choice. I versus you. Me versus them. We see life in an adversarial light now, and the leader as the leading adversary. We haven't just lost consensus, we've deliberately polarized ourselves. Each of us is a majority of one. I and me against the world.

Decades of organization men have spawned, perhaps inevitably, antiorganization men. Junior executives rank their fealty to their own ambitions above any loyalty to the company. And why not? Traditionally, American corporations have seen their employees as adversaries, not allies. Business with a large *B* is the concentrated epitome of our culture, and is inseparable from it. Environmental encroachments and turbulence, the steady beat of litigation, the fragmentation of constituencies, along with their newfound eloquence and power, multiple advocacy, conflicts between internal and external forces, and an everyone-for-him- or herself climate in the executive suites, have turned corporate chiefs into broken field runners—dodging, ducking, moving fast, and demanding "golden parachutes" to soften the inevitable fall.

More and more chiefs, aware of the rancorous mood of the Indians, play it safe and, living up to the inverted proverb, don't just do something but simply sit there. Such people avoid trouble, but they also diminish the possibility of progress. The sense of individual responsibility that animated the Constitution has vanished, as both chiefs and Indians now trumpet the new credos: it's not my job and/or it's not my fault.

In the 1960s, Yippies were political activists. In the 1980s, Yippies are young indicted professionals, while Yuppies, our grand acquisitors, consumed by consumption, turn out to be merely young unindicted professionals—the ones who haven't been caught yet.

Newborn babies are dressed in designer diapers. Little children are pushed into boutique nursery schools, where excellence is measured by the cut of one's polo shirts. Teenagers drive VW Cabriolets and are driven to score stupendously on their SATs, so they can go to Brown with Cosima von Bulow and graduate to Wall Street, where the players use real money, and jail's the only limit.

Young people no longer dream of going to the moon, or even making a better mousetrap. They dream of money, and know that the best things in life—VCRs, cellular phones, Beemers, dinners at the Quilted Giraffe or Rebecca's—aren't free. They don't vote, of course, believing that politics are obsolete, along with politicians.

After the Ivan Boesky insider-trading story broke, a TV news crew went into a Wall Street bar to interview some young traders. To a person, they expressed admiration for Boesky and contempt for the Securities and Exchange Commission. Earlier, when four of their own had been caught playing games that were too fast and loose for even Wall Street, the disgraced young traders were more censured than pitied. Winning isn't everything, it's the only thing, and getting caught is for losers. As one market analyst put it, it isn't either a bull or a bear market anymore, it's a "pig market."

One leading investment banker said that the sight of their colleagues in handcuffs "put the fear of God in everybody," while others merely thanked God that it wasn't them. Such late-inning invocations are standard operating procedure for white-collar felons, as we saw in the wake of Watergate, and why not? Almost anyone would rather wear a halo than handcuffs. New Trinity Church in New York's financial district has opened a center for ethics and corporate policy, but, as the revelations about Jim and Tammy Bakker show, the church is no holier than Wall Street, and, to his credit, Boesky never claimed that God made him do it.

Wall Street's dirty dozen, Bakker's highly secular adventures, and the epidemic of espionage for dollars are the latest manifestations of a social crisis of enormous proportions. Each of us is part talent, part ambition, and part conscience. Ambition accelerates talent, while conscience controls drive and guides talent. Talent and ambition are born and bred in us and are as profoundly personal and distinctive as fingerprints. Conscience is as communal as it is personal, combining our own sense of right and wrong with the prevailing ethic.

In this very material world, the prevailing ethic is at best pragmatic and at worst downright cannibalistic, as corporations eat each other's flesh and sell off the muscle and bones. There's no such thing as the common good or the public interest. There's only self-interest. The old entrepreneurial spirit that Ronald Reagan admires so much has turned anarchic.

Instead of opposing this anarchic turn, far too many public- and private-sector chieftains have opted for a kind of anarchy themselves. The new corporate order disavows fidelity to employees, businesses, factories, communities, the nation, and products. The only things that count to many CEOs are market dominance, profits, and healthy stock prices, according to Steven Prokesch of the *New York Times*. Prokesch writes, "With this mind set, chief executives are losing interest in maintaining a favorable American trade balance, or even manufacturing in America. And they are quick to try out new operating procedures if they seem likely to be profitable. . . . The new corporate thinking casts CEOs as global warriors rather than national ones." In other words, nothing counts except profits, and profits count because they are the sole measure of the CEO. Conscience and competence take a backseat to ambition, as the wheel that turns the fastest gets the bonus.

There was a time when CEOs were civic leaders and corporate statesmen. Today, they have no interest in anything but their own bottom lines. The visionaries, too, are gone. Only surefire products and systems win the attention of the CEO, who has neither the time nor the inclination to commit his or her company to a potentially innovative or even useful product. If it isn't likely to be an instant best-seller, it isn't likely to get an okay. American businessmen never had many moral imperatives, but they did feel some obligation to their employees, the towns they operated in, and the national economy. That's no longer true. In the same way, as Prokesch says, "Many chief executives preach the virtues of employee involvement, teamwork and participative management, but for a calculated reason. Personnel cutbacks have taken a heavy toll on employee loyalty, which, in turn, threatens to take a toll on company efforts to bolster productivity and product quality. As a consequence, executives face the difficult paradox of having to convince employees that they really care about them—until the axe falls in the next wave of cutbacks."

As corporate employers increasingly require their employees to sign "fire-at-will" clauses—statements that the employee recognizes the right of the corporation to fire them "at will," for no fault of their own, for no reason but whim—the last ray of the covenant is dissolving.

Where have all the leaders gone? They're out there pleading, trotting, temporizing, putting out fires, trying to avoid too much heat. They're peering at a landscape of bottom lines. They're money changers lost in a narrow orbit. They resign. They burn out. They decide not to run or serve. They're organizational Houdinis, surrounded by sharks or shackled in a water cage, always managing to escape, miraculously, to make more money via their escape clauses than they made in several years of work. They motivate people through fear, by following trends or by posing as advocates of "reality," which they cynically make up as they go along. They are leading characters in the dreamless society, given now almost exclusively to solo turns.

Thus, precisely at the time when the trust and credibility of our alleged leaders are at an all-time low and when potential leaders feel most inhibited in exercising their gifts, America most needs leaders—because, of course, as the quality of leaders declines, the quantity of problems escalates.

As a person cannot function without a brain, a society cannot function without leaders. And so the decline goes on.

PART THREE

PARTS OF THE PROBLEM

8

Bosses as Heroes
and Celebrities

The captains of industry are back. It's almost impossible to pick up a book or magazine, look at television news (or "Miami Vice," for that matter, which recently featured Lee Iacocca in a cameo bit), or leaf through *People* magazine without getting one more look at America's celebrity executives. In the early 1970s, I lamented the passing of these executive superstars. I have since realized that the reports of their demise were greatly exaggerated. And while it is true that I was one of the first to shout hosanna at their reappearance, I am now reconsidering my initial enthusiasm.

Part of the problem is the sheer volume of uncritical adulation. Crowding my desk as I write this are twin towers of material: books and magazines, and audio and video cassettes, with a sprinkling of brochures and other papers extolling the virtues of corporate leadership. A recent issue of *Psychology Today* reviewed five such books and noted that they "all portray the corporate leader as teacher, mentor, exemplar, and forger of values and meaning." Forget about the Iacocca best-seller or the Peters and Austin book that finally fell from the charts after a solid

365 weeks of best-seller status, only to be replaced by a book about the Fords and the Ford Motor Company. Consider the other books teetering crazily on my desk, such as *The Great Getty* (Lenzner, 1986), *Geneen* (Schoenberg, 1985), Tom Peters's latest offering (subtitled *The Leadership Difference)* (1985), *Making It Happen* (about Olympic CEO Peter Ueberroth) (Reich, 1986), *CEO: Corporate Leadership in Action* (Levinson and Rosenthal, 1984), *The Power to Lead* (Burns, 1984), *The Big Time* (about the extraordinarily successful Harvard Business School class of 1949) (Shames, 1987). There are also books entitled *Leaders* by former president Richard M. Nixon (1982), *Leaders* (Bennis and Nanus, 1985), and *Leader* (Maccoby, 1983). And that's a fraction of the torrent of books celebrating the corporate chieftain as hero.

The way the media describe these new nabobs, I am tempted to exclaim, "Look! Up in the sky! It's a bird. It's a plane. No, it's Superman!" They are described as "incandescent" and almost invariably "charismatic." About GE's Jack Welch: "The Dynamo: tough, tough, and tough. . . . He reaches wildly for a pencil and fresh pad of white lined paper to make ragged sketches . . . they resemble something a toddler might produce, but it doesn't matter; he is already six ideas past them." He's "reinventing GE," according to *Business Week*. About Ted Turner: "As he scrambled to meet a huge debt payment coming due in September, it seemed that Turner was finally about to tumble over the edge. But wait! Embellishing what was already a screwy deal, Turner signed agreements a few weeks ago to sell off MGM assets. . . . That brought him back to the brink. . . . Thus emboldened, Turner would doubtless launch yet another glorious expedition to the edge of oblivion, and another after that" (1986).

The fact is that even my two teenage sons, neither of whom is a business major, recognize the names of Lee Iacocca, T. Boone Pickens, Ted Turner, Armand Hammer, Steve Jobs, Harold Geneen, Victor Kiam, Frank Borman, and Sandy Sigoloff—even if they couldn't name the CEO of Sears. Some of those men are even role models, right up there with Bruce Springsteen—"The Boss."

And that's the important (and disturbing) difference between these captains of industry and their nineteenth-century antecedents. The robber barons were universally hated throughout (and beyond) their lifetimes. Jay Gould was known as "one of the worst stinkers in American business." He once described himself as the "most hated man in America." The other captains of industry fared no better. Given a choice, they would have preferred anonymity to their scandal-wracked lives.

In treating businessmen as icons, we have gone too far in the other direction. The new Man of Steel may not be the most desirable embodiment of "truth, justice, and the American way."

There are some conventional explanations for the re-emergence of the leader as hero in American life. A case can be made, for example, from a strictly business standpoint, that in our turbulent and precarious environment, galloping technology, widespread deregulation, financial and economic upheaval, and social change have combined to complicate vastly the CEO's decision-making process, while raising the stakes and heightening the CEO's visibility. CEOs tend to be more important to troubled companies, so this reasoning goes, and most companies are in trouble in one way or another—if only because they face dramatic change. Another case can be made, strangely contradictory to the first, that this is the most *favorable* climate for business that we have seen in decades—if only because it is the most exhilarating.

A third, discouraging explanation is that, to paraphrase a recently popular song, we are a material people, selfishness is suddenly respectable, and in a nation full of Yuppies bent on acquiring status symbols, there is no higher status or more admirable symbol than the topmost rung on the corporate ladder. A fourth explanation is that in this volatile world, a strong, certain CEO is a far more reliable hero than, say, a rock star.

I prefer another explanation, which goes like this: American cultural traditions define personality, achievement, and the purpose of human life in ways that shower the individual with glory. The chief expounder of this position was Ralph Waldo Emerson (whose famous Phi Beta Kappa address at Harvard,

"On Self-Reliance," was called "our intellectual Declaration of Independence" by Oliver Wendell Holmes). Emerson founded our national literature based on the celebration of "the self." Upon leaving the church, which he referred to as a "mere institution," he gained an individual sense of power that now seems primordial—except when compared to that of an Iacocca or a Pickens.

The dangers of this excessive sense of individual power were described by Alexis de Tocqueville (1980 [1835–1840]), the penetrating observer of American society who invented the word *individualisme*. He wrote: "Americans acquire the habit of always considering themselves as standing alone, and they are apt to imagine their whole destiny is in their hands. Thus not only does democracy make every man forget his ancestors, but it hides descendants, and separates his contemporaries from him; it throws him back upon himself alone, and threatens in the end to confine him entirely within the solitude of his own heart."

Emerson made individualism his religion, disregarding the dangers. For Emerson, society was a problem he waved away, as a pitcher shrugs off a signal from the catcher. Driven to find all his resources, hopes, rewards, and divinity within himself, he ignored philosophical complexities in favor of a rapturous self-affirmation. Power—the crucial aspiration for Emerson—meant the individual's own profound sense of himself, the highest, freest, most abounding and unbridled consciousness. This Emersonian spirit is reflected in the idolatrous goings on right now with regard to leaders. We are in danger of losing individualism's opposite, a sense of community, of collective aspirations, of public service.

When cults develop around leaders, they begin to believe in their own infallibility, and anyone who believes that he or she can do no wrong is a menace to him- or herself as well as to the rest of us. Idolatry turns people into lackeys, so mesmerized by their idol's talents that they neglect their own. Often they are so eager to do their leader's bidding that they don't bother to measure whether what they are doing is right or wrong.

No matter how wise, shrewd, or visionary a leader is, a

corporation is a collective endeavor, and it needs the collective wisdom, canniness, and vision of all its employees to function at the optimum level. These corporate stars eclipse not only their subordinates but also their successors. When a star moves on or retires, the company suffers months, even years, of instability while it searches for someone who can truly fill the star's outsized shoes. Furthermore, these corporate stars imitate their show business counterparts right down to the false retirement and inevitable comeback. CBS's William Paley has already retired several times, and yet he's once again at the helm of the network, to the eternal dismay of several "successors." And A. W. Clausen, despite his mixed reviews, has retaken center stage at Bank of America.

But even when the star does not rise again and again like the phoenix, the company is in for some turbulence as it strains to turn what was a one-man show into a fully functional organization. A monarchy differs from a republic in fundamental ways, and the departed ruler's minions are left with the complex task of picking up the pieces and reassembling them along less autocratic lines.

Whoever takes over the role faces a Herculean task. Those who have inclinations toward stardom themselves have to erase even the memory of their predecessors overnight. Otherwise, they lose face. Those, on the other hand, who choose the path of effective leadership will find that path strewn with hazards, such as executives who have forgotten how to make decisions on their own, a rusted chain of command, and plenty of unfinished business. In such cases, the mortality rate is high. An organization may go through several new CEOs before it finds one who can restore its stability and get it back on course.

Another problem with idolatry is that idols start believing their own press. They behave like mini-emperors, getting rid of dissenters or those who might have better ideas. In addition, emperors naturally have imperial tastes and habits, which tend to cost the company dearly, including perks that would dazzle a sheik, services that are above and beyond the call of both duty and reason, and megabonuses that are not related to the company's profit or loss during the reign. Even after such a person has left the company, the payments continue in the form of stipends, bonuses, and stock. Ironically, the worse such people's performance, the higher their profit is apt to be, since the company is often forced to literally buy them off.

Finally, there is the Oz factor. Far too often, these corporate potentates are empty suits, all sound and show, signifying nothing. This particular breed of star is generally hired under the misapprehension that his or her name or face will bring attention to the company. But it's a bad bargain, as the cost of such a show often exceeds the benefits. Such figureheads frequently lack the kind of experience and knowledge that the corporation requires in its top spot, with the result that it finds itself fumbling while the world stares.

This is not to say that celebrity and performance are mutually exclusive. As in show business, it's possible for a star to be a true talent as well. But high visibility has nothing to do with getting the job done. For example, the no-name executive team at Ford consistently outclasses the stars at Chrysler and General Motors. And the mere presence of a star, talented or not, radically alters whatever arena he or she inhabits, turning otherwise capable associates into fans and skewing everyone's priorities.

When Emerson (certainly both a talent and a star) was at the height of his power and influence, there were detractors who were bothered by his unbridled and insouciant American self. Melville was perhaps the most articulate and mordant: "I do not oscillate in Emerson's rainbow." Emerson wished to give people courage to be, to follow their own instincts—and this became the platform for American enterprise and a philosophical license for great corporate tycoons. What he failed to realize was that these unchecked instincts can be rapacious. Or, in the nineteenth-century idiom of William Henry Vanderbilt, "The public be damned."

In today's adoration not of the magi but of the CEOs, the public seems not to care that it is being damned, that not only the T. Boone Pickenses and the Carl Icahns but even the Lee Iacoccas are building their individual power bases at the expense of the greater community. Emerson and his latter-day disciples never seemed to grasp that a social fabric exists for the protection of its members, as do the laws and inhibitions that such a fabric demands. He did not create American expansionism and our special exploitative verve, but he did give them a blessing and a high-minded boost. We must be vigilant that we don't oscillate too long in Emerson's rainbow.

9

When There Are
Too Many Chiefs

In the beginning, organizations were exceedingly simple. There were chiefs and tribes, or kings and subjects, or owners and tenants, or bosses and workers. With the advent of the Industrial Revolution, it got more complicated. There were stockholders, boards of directors, officers, and employees. Now it's too complicated—with stakeholders and/or shareholders, chairs of the boards and/or CEOs, corporate presidents and/or COOs, assorted vice-presidents, managers, and employees. Naturally, the modern organization, being complicated, even byzantine, is much more subject to trouble and breakdowns than its predecessors were.

As a rule, such organizational breakdowns occur in the privacy of corporate executive suites, but the whole world got to see a classic example of structural failure during the 1987 White House power struggle, which climaxed with President Ronald Reagan firing his chief of staff, Donald Regan. The president was rapped for his "managerial style," but actually the problems resided in his managerial mode. Reagan and Regan learned the hard way that there are more weaknesses than strengths in the two-track CEO-COO mode.

76

Given its political bias, the Reagan administration's choice of a corporate structure over a bureaucratic chain of command was reasonable, as was the appointment of Regan, a top business executive, as chief of staff. But Regan's view of his role was anything but reasonable and was the basis for the subsequent fire storm. Though as chief of staff, Regan was the White House equivalent of a COO serving CEO Reagan, from the outset he behaved like a CEO, usurping both Reagan's authority and his prerogatives. COOs are secondary, not primary, spokespersons, yet Regan issued frequent off-the-cuff pronouncements, which were often at odds with his boss's policies and pronouncements. Furthermore, COO Regan isolated CEO Reagan from both his staff and his constituents, which resulted in the CEO seeing the world more and more through his COO's lens.

Finally, of course, the flaws in the two men's relationship magnified the flaws inherent in the structure and brought it all down, and Regan, the quintessential corporate boss, was replaced by Howard Baker, the quintessential bureaucratic team player. As something like order returned to the White House, Iran and Contragate notwithstanding, there must have been sympathetic sighs and nods in corporate headquarters all over America, because no one knows better how flawed and how basically unworkable the CEO-COO power split is than the CEOs and COOs themselves.

Contemporary corporate structure is, at best, a jerry-built rig, which emerged out of perceived need and chance rather than choice, and like every fragile, sensitive machine, it's only as good as its parts. The principal parts of the corporate machine are people, and people come to the job at hand with all their own sensitivities, fragilities, and needs. And the higher a person rises in the corporate hierarchy, the more exposed his or her strengths and weaknesses are. Nowhere are these strengths and weaknesses more exposed and more tested than in the relationship between a CEO and his COO.

On paper, the differences between the two jobs are very clear. The CEO is the leader, the COO the manager. The CEO is charged with doing the right thing, the COO with doing things right. The CEO takes the long view, the COO the short view. The CEO concentrates on the what and why, while the COO focuses on how. The CEO has the vision, the COO hands-on control. The CEO thinks in terms of innovation, development, the future, while the COO is busy with administration, maintenance, the present. The CEO sets the tone and direction, both inside and outside the company, while the COO sets the pace. Ironically, as with Reagan and Regan, even when the CEO and COO function happily together, they can run into big trouble, as mutual admiration is not necessarily relevant, much less productive. But when they're unhappy together, their unhappiness is reflected throughout the organization in major and minor ways, which leads to trouble, too.

No one makes it into the upper reaches of the corporate world without a very healthy ego and very strong opinions about everything. Given this, even the most serene CEO (which may be an oxymoron) is bound to occasionally envy the COO's hands-on control, while the COO must long sometimes to think ahead, dream, innovate. The logic here is that two heads are better than one, but I don't know any top executives who, in their heart of hearts, don't think that their own heads are better than all the other heads put together.

In addition to these fundamental problems, there are other traps in the structure. What the CEO imagines, the COO makes manifest—often in ways that seem wrong to the CEO. Then, too, the COO seems the natural heir to the CEO and, if there were any real sense in this structure, would be. But COO skills, which are primarily managerial, are not necessarily useful in the CEO slot, which requires a leader's talents, so a superb manager can move into the leader's chair and find him- or herself back at square one, scrambling to learn a whole new game and often striking out.

If the COO opposes the CEO, no matter how valid that position, one time or twenty times, the COO may jeopardize his or her ultimate ascension. This may serve to intimidate or inhibit the COO, making him or her both a less effective COO and a less likely CEO candidate.

Obviously, all COOs come to the job with their own managerial style, and, if they are any good at all, they have both knowledge of and ideas about their company and the desire to use their knowledge to the full and express their ideas freely. If they don't see eye to eye with their CEOs, they can either challenge them or remain silent. If the COO challenges the CEO, the COO may, depending on both the wisdom of the challenge and the character of the CEO, risk incurring the enmity of the CEO, which means that his or her days are probably numbered as COO, and the chances of ever getting the top job are nil.

On the other hand, COOs who remain silent do both themselves and the company a disservice. The moment any executive begins to tailor his or her ideas and performance to suit the boss, that executive is diminished, and, because no CEO is infallible, the company may lose, too. In addition, any time a COO, or any other top executive, deliberately trims the sails, withholding ideas or energy from the company, he or she simultaneously reduces his or her own opportunities for advancement.

Donald Regan's downfall was a direct result of his assuming too much authority and too little responsibility. He spoke too much for the president and too little to him, withholding any ideas or information that were at odds with his own. If he had been less a censor and more of a critic, Regan might still be in the White House.

COOs, then, are constantly between a rock and a hard place, damned if they do and damned if they don't. Their first loyalty must always be to the company. It, after all, pays them very well and expects them to give 100 percent on the job. But if they give 100 percent, applying all their knowledge, experience, and expertise, they may find themselves on the outs with the CEO who, for good reason or no reason at all, feels threatened by the second in command.

The two-track CEO-COO structure is so susceptible to problems because, at bottom, it's unworkable. However clean and clear the division of responsibilities is on paper, in practice these responsibilities are indivisible, inextricably interwoven. Every leader has something of the manager, and every top manager has qualities of leadership and otherwise probably would not have made it to the top. Thus, the CEO wears both leadership and managerial hats and is bound to tread on the COO's turf at least occasionally. At the same time, the COO can't resist flexing those leader's muscles occasionally and assuming some of the CEO's prerogatives.

In the same line, the conscientious COO wants not merely to do things right but to do the right thing, and wants, too, to occasionally take the long view. Indeed, it is impossible not to take the long view sometimes.

The solution to the CEO-COO dilemma is as simple as the structure is complex. The key responsibilities of both the CEO and COO should be combined and assigned to a CEO in chief, who would reside at the center of a kind of constellation of executives. This CEO in chief would be the leader and the manager of managers, each of whom would superintend a portion of the company's operations. The CEO would be expected to do the right thing, enabling the managers to do things right, and would be responsible for seeing that the short view was compatible with the long view, that things done today would lead to tomorrow's goals. He or she would define the whats and whys and assign the hows to associates; would have the vision and primary hands-on control, thus ensuring that the vision was always realistic; would think in terms of innovation, development, and the future, while his or her associates took care of administration, maintenance, and the present; and would set tone, direction, and pace. Since the division of these various tasks was arbitrary, even accidental, their reunion would make for a generally more effective, efficient operation, along with eliminating the possibility of CEO-COO conflicts.

Since the CEO in chief's assistants would possess both the requisite managerial and leadership skills and talents and would gain broad experience working with and for their CEO, some would be likely candidates for the top spot. The CEO in chief would be limited to a seven-year term—to ensure against burnout, complacency, or any of the other afflictions CEOs are now heir to.

With less structure and more leadership, American business might begin to recover its verve, energy, and spunk. But, for the moment, anyway, not only is there little demand for verve, energy, and spunk in the nation's executive suites, there is an unnatural and unhealthy affection for the status quo.

10

Bottom-Line Obsessions

When GE took over RCA in 1986, it was comparable to a whale swallowing another whale. GE had had an impressive several years, but RCA not only had had an equally impressive run lately; it was, thanks to its highly visible subsidiary, NBC, better known and more influential than GE.

It was not ever thus. A few years ago, NBC was a wreck of a network, but it won the 1985–86 rating wars, easily besting ABC, along with the once-imperial CBS, and repeated its stunning performance in the 1986–87 season. It won nearly every week, leading runner-up CBS by two full rating points, which translates into approximately three million homes and millions of dollars in ad revenues. Analysts expected the television network to enjoy a sharp increase in operating profit from the $202.5 million it earned in 1987 on revenues of about $2.2 billion. To its further credit, NBC has made this impressive advance not by pandering to the worst in its audience but by challenging it with new kinds of programming, often brilliantly conceived and wrought. It has, then, managed to combine financial success with substantive product innovations and improvements.

The principal architect of NBC's amazing renaissance,

Grant Tinker, left the network shortly after GE took over, and, ironically, his successor, Robert Wright, a longtime GE hand, seems determined, at the very least, to pluck the peacock. Shortly after taking over, he asked each network division to come up with a plan to reduce its budget by 5 percent. That's standard operating procedure for GE, whose CEO, Jack Welch, is called Neutron Jack, because when he finishes "streamlining" a company, the buildings remain but the people are gone. Unfortunately, what's SOP for GE may turn out to be fatal to the peacock, and the difference between Tinker's leadership and GE-style management is almost a casebook study on the differences between bold entrepreneurship and timid management.

In the last several years, the networks have lost viewers to more aggressive independent TV stations, cable TV, and video cassette recorders, and so ad revenues are flat or down. If revenues don't grow, and moderate inflation continues, along with such built-in cost increases as contractually binding salary increases, obviously the network's profits will begin to decline, or so Wright believes. He told the *New York Times*, "From my standpoint, we have no choice but to look at the same future ABC and CBS are looking at. In the next 18 to 24 months, without advertising growth and only moderate inflation, we will not be able to do any better than we've done. Our organization has to understand that in order to have a successful business in five years."

Wrong, Mr. Wright. First, it was Tinker's insistence on seeing a future different from the one that ABC and CBS saw that led to NBC's renaissance and ABC's and CBS's simultaneous declines. Second, a successful network, like any other business, is only as successful as its product. A TV network's only product is programs, and at NBC, according to one executive, of the two thousand West Coast employees, fewer than fifty are directly involved in the creation and development of programs. In this light, an across-the-board reduction of 5 percent seems not merely foolish but blind. If anything, the programming division should be encouraged to increase its budget by at least 5 percent.

Faced with disastrous ratings and pitiful revenues when he took over, Tinker became the very model of an entrepreneur.

First, he understood that the principal capital now is human capital, and he encouraged the most creative people in the business to come to NBC with their ideas. Second, he understood that the key to generating new wealth is innovation, and, working with NBC's chief programmer, Brandon Tartikoff, he brought us a new kind of TV—a cop show without car chases, another cop show in which the look and the sound are as vital as guns and bad guys, and comedies about an alcoholic bartender, four over-the-hill ladies, and a black middle-class family.

"Hill Street Blues," "Miami Vice," "Cheers," "Golden Girls," and "The Cosby Show," along with such other NBC innovations as "St. Elsewhere," in which the doctors and nurses are as vulnerable as their patients, and "L.A. Law," in which the lawyers are as beset as their clients, *are* contemporary TV—beautifully crafted and performed, sophisticated, innovative, and sometimes controversial. With the exception of "The Cosby Show," which may be the most popular TV series of all time, none of these models of TV excellence was an instant hit, but Tinker and Tartikoff stuck by them, in the best entrepreneurial fashion. Tinker didn't follow the audience, he led it, and remade it, along with network television itself.

Faced with winning ratings and soaring revenues when he took over, Wright has been the very model of a dutiful manager, never looking beyond the bottom line, more concerned with cutting costs than improving the product, eschewing innovation, and, above all, ranking careful management over creative entrepreneurship. The moment that he took over, Wright abandoned his predecessor's daring entrepreneurial approach, choosing instead the posture of the reflexive manager, and thus seemed bent on turning the leader into a follower. ABC and CBS were cutting back, so NBC must cut back, too.

In defense of this odd tack, which might be described as following the losers, Wright said, "GE and Bob Wright will have failed if we wait until NBC stumbles and then try to fix it." But, of course, the way to keep NBC on top is to continue developing innovative programming, to move forward, not cut back. Instead of managing NBC's money, Wright should be encouraging its talented programmers and the pool of creative pro-

ducers, writers, and performers drawn to NBC by Tinker and
Tartikoff.

Wright said, "Cost and profitability are not necessarily related. You can't guarantee ways to get market share and you
can't guarantee ways to keep it. The business is governed by intangibles: viewer tastes, competition, affiliate relations. There is
a lack of clarity about where you're going." In fact, Tinker
knew exactly where he was going. He knew that if NBC gave the
audience programs that were genuinely new and different, as
well as being beautifully crafted, it would not only attract but
hold the audience's attention. If there is now "a lack of clarity"
about where NBC is going, it has been triggered by Wright himself. In addition to laying off 150 people and heading another
150 toward early retirement following NBC's best year ever,
and asking division heads to come up with the 5 percent budget
cuts, he also scolded administrators for overly cautious "belt-
and-suspenders" management (though he seems the archetypal
belt-and-suspenders man himself) and suggested that NBC start
a political action committee funded with employee contributions. To this point, it seems that GE man Wright is determined
to turn out the lights at NBC. But, of course, he's playing to an
audience of one, his boss, Jack Welch, whom he wants to succeed. However, it is worth noting that only two NBC chiefs
have ever left the post voluntarily. One was Robert Sarnoff, son
of the company's founder. The other was Tinker.

Tinker, not coincidentally, turned down an offer from
Wright to buy a piece of Tinker's new production company, in
order to ensure his continuing connection with NBC. Instead,
Tinker has signed a program deal with CBS, with the avowed
purpose of "blowing right by" NBC in the ratings. Grant Tinker/
Gannett Entertainment (GTG), in addition to its deal with CBS,
has $40 million in the bank and a studio with twelve sound
stages in Culver City, California, along with several seasoned and
esteemed creative TV veterans, all of whom were in place before
much thought was given to a business affairs specialist.

One Wall Street analyst said appreciatively of Wright,
"He's trying to bring the real world into focus at NBC." What
neither Wright nor the analyst understands is that Tinker

brought the "real world" to NBC six years ago, when he determined that if he brought the best creative people to the network and gave them the time, money, and leeway to do their best, then the network would thrive. He was right. Network profits increased tenfold during his tenure, TV programming was revolutionized, and NBC's hit shows won critical acclaim and countless Emmys, along with ratings.

Admittedly, Tinker is a tough act to follow, but it's the only act that works in the real world. Entrepreneurs such as Tinker know that human capital is the only capital that really counts now. Managers such as Wright who have spent their corporate lives watching the bottom line still haven't got the message. Wright is, in fact, a sterling example of George Santayana's dictum that those who do not learn from history are doomed to repeat it. In the late 1970s, Transamerica bought United Artists and tried to apply the "efficiencies" of the insurance business to running a movie studio. Arthur Krim, Michael Medavoy, and their associates left to form Orion Pictures, and Transamerica had nothing but a shell of a studio and a film library. Orion is now a major studio, and Transamerica is out of the film business.

It has been American big business's obsession with the bottom line in the last decade and its continuing inability to see that its workers are its primary asset that has got it into such trouble. Until the Tinkers outnumber the Wrights, America is destined to continue to lag, in vital ways, in the volatile world market.

11

Untapped Human Capital

Louis B. Mayer, the head of MGM Studios during Hollywood's golden era, was known for his tyrannical habits, yet he made MGM into a pivotal cultural force, shaping the movies that shaped America. He knew what today's corporate titans either never knew or can't accept, that the only capital that really counts is human capital.

Mayer once said, "The inventory goes home at night," conceding, however inelegantly, that without his corps of talented directors, writers, and actors, MGM would be nothing. In the same way, whatever a modern corporation markets, from cars to meals to life insurance, its primary resource is its people. This is a basic economic fact, and it is the American business-people's refusal to accept and act on it that accounts, to a large degree, for America's poor performance in the international marketplace.

American business has traditionally seen its workers in an adversarial light, as mere cogs in the corporate machine: necessary, perhaps, but anonymous, replaceable, and greedy. In the first decades of the Industrial Revolution, workers were treated as indentured servants. Finally, of course, the workers rebelled, and, by the middle of this century, a kind of uneasy peace was established, with unions and businesses in approximate if rancorous balance. But today, there is far more rancor than balance.

The country's top CEO, Ronald Reagan, expressed the basic animosity that too many CEOs feel toward both unions and workers when he fired the air traffic controllers. Nobody plays a more crucial role in the airlines' operations than air traffic controllers. Our lives are literally in their hands, but the president nonetheless saw them as expendable and got rid of them, because they dared to ask for salaries that were commensurate with their responsibilities.

As the president went, so went corporate America. We have entered into a period of union bashing that is unprecedented in modern times. In the 1980s, workers are not only undervalued, they are scapegoats. As American business lost its comfortable edge in the international market, American businesspeople blamed allegedly lazy and careless workers. In fact, the problems resided, for the most part, in the executive suites. American executives had themselves got lazy and careless.

The bottom line wasn't everything, it was the only thing. Profits mattered more than products. Making money was more important than making quality goods. It wasn't until profits began to decline that American businesspeople even noticed that something had gone awry, and then, in time-honored fashion, they began laying off workers and shutting down plants. They had not even enough vision to see that they were losing to their overseas competition because their products, not their workers, were inferior, and their products were inferior because they devoted far more energy to making short-term profits than to developing innovative, functional, and useful products. Now they are nearly out of the game. America still leads in research and development, thanks to its natural store of talented, imaginative workers, but it trails in manufacturing and marketing, thanks to its lack of talent and imagination in the executive suites. Furthermore, the most impressive R&D goes on in small new companies, which have replaced the traditional adversarial posture with a freewheeling cooperative spirit.

These successful new companies are run not like feudal estates, in which workers are expected to be seen and never

heard, but like round tables, in which workers not only are expected to speak up but are assured of a receptive audience. In
this way, all the talents of all the workers are tapped and used
to the benefit of everyone, including company customers. What's
more, these businesses are profitable and are adding workers,
even as *Fortune* 500 companies are losing money and laying off
workers. Like Mayer, the heads of these young companies know
that their primary resource is people. They understand that
healthy, spirited people are the primary source of economic
growth. Research shows that since 1928 the principal source of
new or added national income has been human resources. Power
and profit used to reside in property. Now they reside in people;
and that key measure productivity, in both companies and nations, is attributable less to the quantity of their resources than
to the quality of their people.

Everyone seems to understand this fundamental fact of
business life except our business titans. In a pastoral letter released in late 1986, "Economic Justice for All: Catholic Social
Teaching and the U.S. Economy," the National Conference of
Catholic Bishops (1986) showed more business savvy than many
CEOs. Noting that "The promise of the American dream—freedom for all persons to develop their God-given talents to the
full—remains unfulfilled for millions in the United States today," and concerned about the "social fragmentation, a decline
in seeing how one's work serves the whole community," the
bishops called for "new forms of cooperation and partnership
among those whose daily work is the source of prosperity and
justice of the nation . . . for new structures of economic partnership and participation within firms." But, the bishops
warned, "Partnerships between labor and management are possible only when both groups possess real freedom and power to
influence decisions."

Unfortunately, such partnerships, however sensible, seem
unlikely. Even in the young, successful companies, we can already see signs of the traditional hierarchical habits cropping
up. As these small new companies grow, they look more and
more like the big old companies, and the same old schisms develop between bosses and workers. One can only conclude that

the American businessperson is uniquely susceptible to hubris. It seems to come with the territory.

If these arrogant American chieftains do not begin to see the world as it is, do not finally acknowledge that their employees are their primary asset, not their primary liability, then all their jealously held power, prerogatives, and perks will sooner or later count for nothing, because their companies will be acquired, merged, or sunk.

12

The Perils of Accord

When Texan Ross Perot sold his Electronics Data Systems to General Motors several years ago, it looked like a dream merger: a star in the new technological industry amalgamating with one of the nation's oldest and most esteemed corporations. But, as in many May-December marriages, the dream went quickly sour. In late 1986, Perot was ousted from the GM board and his position as chair of EDS, bought out of GM for some $700 million, and, under his buyout agreement, obliged to pay up to $7.5 million in fines if he publicly criticized GM.

The ouster and the buyout were triggered by Perot's continuing criticism of GM officers and his opposition to year-end bonuses. This astonishing turn raises some basic questions about corporate management. What distinguishes effective executives from ineffective ones? How do corporations remain alive and alert, unblinded by their own successes, undamaged by their failures?

The rift between Perot, who built his company from nothing, and GM chair Roger Smith began when the self-made man was publicly critical of the organization men at GM in particular and in the American corporate world in general. He alleged that American executives should stop blaming unfair foreign competition and lazy production workers for their problems. At a press conference in December, he said, "We spent nearly $40 billion over the last several years and lost market share. During that time we've gone from the low-cost producer to the high-cost producer. Now, I'm just saying we've been doing something here that's not producing an end result" (*New Management*, 1987, pp. 62–63).

He continued, "Here is my frustration. We're the biggest, we've got the greatest dealer network in the world. We've got more human resources than anyone in the world. We're spending $3.6 billion a year on [research and development]. Gosh, we ought to have a car that can ice-skate. We've got more of everything than anybody. But when you look at the results, we've got Chrysler, a fourth our size, who is the low cost producer. There's something wrong. We just closed 11 plants, laid off 30,000 people, and we just threw $700 million at a guy who didn't want it." In speaking of the bonuses he opposed, Perot said, "You should take care of the guys who do the work and then the guys that run the place. You can't . . . say it has been a bad year, we can't do anything for you, but then say, 'By the way, we are going to pay ourselves a million-dollar bonus over here.'"

Obviously, "the guys that run the place" disagreed with Perot. They tossed him out and paid themselves the bonus. If a poll were taken of top executives, it's likely that the majority of them would side with Smith and his cohorts. Which raises another question: Do corporations in this volatile era function more effectively on accord or discord?

I happen to think that too much accord is always perilous and usually false. Two of this country's most effective executives, Jim Burke at Johnson & Johnson and Andrew Grove at Intel, insist on what they describe as "creative confrontation" with their associates. They not only encourage dissent in the executive suite, they demand it, and they surround themselves with people smart enough to know the truth and independent enough to speak it—especially when it's at apparent odds with their own perceptions.

If corporate officers are to function in the real world,

then they have to live and work in the real world, never insulating or isolating themselves or surrounding themselves with people too much like themselves. One of the causes of Richard Nixon's fall was his reliance on men who were merely clones of himself. They couldn't tell him anything he didn't already know and so were useless to him.

Just as they expect dissent, disagreement, and truth from their associates, effective executives go in search of the truth themselves, spending considerable time in the field, looking at their own operations, talking with their workers and their customers. The great German composer and conductor Gustav Mahler insisted that each principal musician in the orchestra sit in the audience at least once a week to get some sense of the whole.

Effective executives, no matter how high they rise, remain inquisitive, curious about everything. They read, go around, look, explore, wonder, make connections, always know that their company is not the whole but only part of it. They are by nature restless, never satisfied, ever aware that there is no such thing as perfection, convinced that any product can be improved and any procedure upgraded. Furthermore, effective executives know that the world is not static but dynamic, in a constant state of flux. They do not believe in the status quo but are committed to change. GM, along with many other major American companies, got complacent. Sales were good, profits were healthy. If they had a maxim, it was "If it ain't broke, don't fix it," and then the Japanese and Germans came along, and nearly broke them.

Effective executives' priorities are very clear, and, appropriately enough, the bottom line is the last thing on their minds, while the first order of business is customer satisfaction. Customer satisfaction derives from good products and services, which in turn derive from talented, committed workers. Satisfied customers, talented committed workers, first-rate products and services inevitably add up and make the company profitable, but effective executives continue to look and listen in an effort to see, hear, and understand the world as it is, and as it is becoming. Corporations remain alive and alert and unblinded by their own success, then, to the degree that the people in charge remain alive and alert to the world. It's that simple, and that complicated.

In buying Perot off, Smith and his minions effectively silenced the messenger, but the message is still loud and clear. GM's lack of real leadership has cost dearly. Smith's subsequent decision to eliminate the annual bonuses was too little and too late and was further proof of his inability to lead his embattled company out of its self-imposed troubles.

13

The Pornography of Leadership

When the Pentagon Papers were published (Bantam Books, 1971) over government objections in the early 1970s, what disturbed me even more than the deceits, the counterdeceits, the moral numbness and ethical short-circuiting of our leaders was the pornography of it all, the hubris of those men in the White House and the Pentagon, thousands of miles away from Vietnam, making life-and-death decisions for others, manipulating the most modern tools of technology, using game theory with models so abstract they could reproduce one another in one joyless, screaming parthenogenetic act. But not once could these men experience the epiphany of childbirth—or the smell of burning flesh.

I thought of pornography because that also is distanced from reality, from direct experience. Actors in porn films are not real people making love but appendages of sexual organs engaged in mechanical acts. These appendages are so without personalities or identifiable social characteristics that, as one movie critic pointed out, they are more about physical engineering than love—just so many pistons and valves. Loveless sex. Distant, remote, calculated, vicarious. The "war room" at the Pentagon is as distant from the reality of war as downtown Boston's so-called "combat zone," the festooned, free area for porno sales, is from the reality of sex.

In the Pentagon Papers, we see Secretary of Defense Robert S. McNamara busying himself with the minutiae of war planning, because lists of numbers and cost estimates have a distracting if illusory moral neutrality. Toward the end of his tenure, he stops questioning the military or political significance of sending 206,000 more troops into Indochina, into a war he now knows cannot be won, and concentrates instead on the logistical problems of getting them there. That's administration. And his wife reports that, as he fulfilled the requirements of efficiency and effectiveness during his own final days, he began to grind his teeth—every night—while tossing fitfully.

The so-called "good Nazi" (certainly an oxymoron) Albert Speer elevated the promises of Hitler's "technocracy" to a point where those promises quickly became shields against any inclination to think of the human and social consequences of his actions. The challenges, the deadlines, the deadly routines of the Third Reich—as of the Defense Department or any large bureaucracy—become tasks to be performed, power to be exercised, problems to be solved, monuments to be designed (or demolished).

Is it the nature of large-scale organizations that makes it possible for an ethical person such as a McNamara, as well as unethical Irangaters, to work toward an ultimately immoral end without an immediate sense of personal responsibility or guilt? Bureaucracies are, by definition, systems of increased differentiation and specialization, and thus the ultimate morality of bureaucracy is the amorality of segmented acts.

On the first real day of spring in 1976, when I was president of the University of Cincinnati, two beautiful trees in the infancy of bloom were chopped down to make more room for cars to turn down a campus driveway. Everybody was outraged. Students packed into my office to tell me about it. A few were hysterical and crying. I left my office and walked over to the little grass plot—there was so little green on the campus—where

I saw a man with a small hand saw, cleaning and stacking up the milk-white wood into neat piles.

A crowd of some 200 students and faculty stood around, and, as I broke through the circle to speak to the man with the saw, I heard hissing. He said, "Man, am I glad you're here. They're ready to crucify me." It turned out that he wasn't employed by the university but worked for a local contractor. I never found out who was responsible: the landscape artist who designed the new plot with poodle hedges or his boss, the landscape architect; the director of planning or his boss, the head of the physical plant; the vice-president for management and finance, the university building committee, the executive vice-president the committee reports to. . . . When I called them all together, they numbered twenty, and they were innocents all. All of us. Bureaucracies are beautiful mechanisms for the evasion of responsibility and guilt. Too far from the classroom, from the munitions plant, from the battlefield, from the people, from love. That's pornography.

There are no easy answers—or options. The problem is immense and invades all of our lives. According to the Census Bureau, fewer than 2 percent of us are self-employed now. Everyone else works in large organizations. In the 1900s, it was the opposite ratio. And it's simplistic and unrealistic to talk about "small is beautiful," as we learned in the 1970s. Smallness helps only if it prevents the episodic, disconnected experience that characterizes so many of our leaders and administrators, but it usually doesn't, because increasingly they're the products of bigness. Nor does it solve anything when a leader pretends closeness to or a direct relationship with the people, as when Jimmy Carter wore jeans and cardigan sweaters in the White House. The "simple" life—as seen on a technotronic quadraphonic TV tube—is soft porn for the intellectual, falsely soothing and just as corrupt as the hard kind.

What's important, it seems to me, is the capacity to see things in wide perspective, to receive impressions and gain experiences directly, not vicariously, impressions that point beyond the experiences and data themselves—continuity and purpose.

To the pornographic leader, things and events of the world appear as portable fragments. The long view is replaced by shortsightedness. There is detail but no pattern. The fresh outlook yields to a stereotyped and biased one. Experiences and impressions, what there are of them seen through the lucite grey of a limousine window, cannot be fully valued and enjoyed because their character—their feel, their smell, their grit—is lost.

One of the reasons that Ronald Reagan and his kitchen cabinet sometimes seem so out of touch with the real world is that they are out of touch—insulated by position, money, and circumstance from what goes on in the streets of America or, for that matter, the kitchens. Our leaders must reacquaint themselves with the world, must explore in the presence of others, must reach out and touch the people they presume to lead, and must, occasionally at least, risk making a mistake rather than doing nothing. In the meantime, they will continue to sound as if they were talking through a plate-glass window—distant, isolated, removed from the complex lives of living people.

14

When Winning Is Losing

Americans are, on the whole, simple and direct people. Unlike Europeans, we do not incline toward nuances or subtleties, in either our lives or our work. Unlike Asians, we opt inevitably for the concrete over the abstract. We are also extremely competitive, relishing our opponents' losses as exuberantly as we boast of our own victories. For these reasons, sports are not only our favorite form of entertainment but our principal model and metaphor for our own lives.

At home, at work, we talk of winning and losing, scoring touchdowns, carrying the ball, close calls, going down to the wire, batting a thousand, making a hole in one, being behind the eight ball, and while we may like movie, TV, and rock stars, we admire sports stars. Every father wants his sons to shine on the playing fields, which is why Little League games frequently have all the carefree air of the London blitz.

Preachers and politicians, among others, see this national obsession as healthy, portray us as good, clean people interested in good, clean fun. Universities, including my own, celebrate and reward their hero-athletes. On the day of the Super Bowl, the entire country's collective consciousness is focused on The Game.

I am admittedly as obsessed as anyone. I can remember great plays, great players, even scores of great games forever, though I sometimes can't remember whom I sat next to at dinner three nights ago. But I am also convinced that it's time to find a new model. Life is not a baseball game. It's never called on account of darkness, much less canceled because of inclement weather. And while major sports are big business now, business is not a sport, and never was. Indeed, thinking of business as a kind of game or sport was always simplistic. Now it's downright dangerous.

A game is of limited duration, takes place on or in a fixed and finite site, is governed by openly promulgated rules, as defined in books that are available to everyone and enforced on the spot by neutral professionals, and is performed by more or less evenly matched teams who are counseled and guided through every move by seasoned hands. Scores are kept, and, at the end of the game, a winner is declared. If there is anyone out there who can say that his or her business is of limited duration, takes place on a fixed site, is governed by openly promulgated rules, as defined in books that are available to everyone and enforced on the spot by neutral professionals, competes only with more or less evenly matched businesses, and can describe its wins and losses in absolute terms, then that person is either extraordinarily lucky or seriously deluded.

The risks of thinking of business in sports terms are numerous. First, to measure a business on the basis of wins and losses is to misunderstand both the purposes of a specific business and the nature of business itself. No business—whether it sells insurance or manufactures cars—can or should be designed to win. It must rather be designed to grow, on both quantitative and qualitative levels. In this sense, it vies more with itself than with its competition. This is not to say that in head-to-head contests, as when two ad agencies are competing for the same account, there are not winners and losers. It is to say, in paraphrase of Vince Lombardi's legendary dictum, that winning isn't everything; it's one of many things a business must accomplish. Thus, a company that's designed merely to win is bound to lose. For example, John Doe Insurance could win the auto insurance market overnight by offering total-coverage policies at, say, $100 per year, but when the claims began coming in, John Doe would lose his shirt.

Second, it's perilous to think of limits, rules, and absolutes in business. Athletes compete for a given number of hours in a given number of games over a given period of weeks or months. Businesses are in the arena for decades, even centuries. Though the action may rise and subside, it never stops. It doesn't offer any time-outs, much less neatly defined beginnings and endings. As they say, it isn't over until it's over.

American business has traditionally been schizophrenic about rules. When it's flourishing, it wants no rules or regulations. When it's failing, it wants a plethora of rules. Some of the airlines that lobbied most vigorously for deregulation have now, ironically, gone down in flames, victims of the very instrument they agitated for. In the same way, Detroit saw Washington as its nemesis, until foreign cars began to take over the market. Suddenly, Chrysler went to the feds for a loan, and now Detroit begs Washington to regulate the imports but continues to lobby against federal safety and quality controls.

Athletes perform in a static environment—the size of the field, the length of the contest, even the wardrobes of the players remain the same day after month after year. Businesses function in a volatile universe, which changes from moment to moment and hardly ever repeats. It is affected by droughts half a world away, a new gismo down the street, consumer attitudes and needs, a million things. Given this mercurial context, any business that is not at least as dynamic and flexible as the world in which it functions will soon be out of step or out of business.

Clearly, then, there are far more differences than similarities between sports and business. But the real danger in the sports model is not its bad match but its bad example. The best-run and most successful companies in America do not think in terms of victories and defeats, or shining moments, or last-minute saves, and do not count on regulations or referees. Instead, they think in terms of staying power, dedication to quality, and an endless effort to do better than they have done (which might, of course, be said of our top athletes and teams, too), and they see change as their only constant, count on their own ability to adapt to the world, rather than expecting the world to adapt to them. Indeed, it is a business's ability to adapt to an ever-changing world that is the basis for both its success and its progress.

The truth is that there is no workable or appropriate model for business except business itself, and that should be sufficient. Like a well-played game, a well-run business is something to see, but, unlike a well-played game, it is not a diversion, it is life itself—complex, difficult, susceptible to both success and failure, sometimes unruly, always challenging, and often joyful.

15

The Name of the Game Is Greed

Today, accountants and celebrities seem to be running American business, and some demented fringe seems to be in charge of the government. Our foreign policy is apparently in the hands of minor but zealous functionaries, and we've had no coherent domestic policy for a decade, because it's easier to write off the poor than to bring them back into society. Thus, America—having been invented by brilliant political leaders and developed by brilliant business leaders—has no leaders at all today. Instead, we have gamesmen—men and women who are vastly clever and ambitious but have no real understanding or vision.

It was the gamesmen who invented Ronald Reagan, of course, and he has suited them to a T, not because he is wise or strong, or even charming and amiable, but because he has said again and again—implicitly and explicitly—that it's okay to be selfish. With Ron's blessing, they just went for the gold, without fear of censure. After two hundred years, it's finally official: democracy is out, and capitalism is in.

The problem is, we've lost the Midas touch. America's gamesmen are not any better at capitalism than they were at

102

democracy. Unable to deal with the competition from abroad, the gamesmen have cried foul and demanded protectionist legislation. With no holds barred, megacorporations consume other megacorporations. The gamesmen who set up these megadeals win, while everyone else loses. The Dow Jones average more and more resembles a roller coaster as the game goes on.

The name of the game is greed, of course, and it's a fool's game, but as long as the gamesmen are in charge, it's all we've got.

PART FOUR

PARTS OF
THE SOLUTION

16

Leading to Make a Difference

When asked what wisdom the ancient Oriental philosophers could pass along to modern humanity, Ralph Siu offered a list of "advices." One went as follows: "Observe the cormorant in the fishing fleet. You know how cormorants are used for fishing. The technique involves a man in a rowboat with about a half-dozen cormorants, each with a ring about its neck. When the bird spots a fish, it dives into the water and catches the fish in its beak. The ring prevents the larger fish from being swallowed, so the fisherman takes the fish from the cormorant, which then dives for another fish."

Why is it, Siu asked, of all the animals, the cormorant has been chosen to slave away for the fisherman? If the bird were not greedy for the fish, efficient in catching it, and readily trainable, would society have created an industry to exploit it? Or would the ingenious ring have been devised? Of course not. Thus, Siu concludes, greed, talent, and capacity for learning become the bases for exploitation. Institutions and organizations are designed to make society, not the individual, prosper. Therefore, society encourages greed, talent, and the capacity for learning in us, then puts rings around our necks and makes cormorants of us.

How can we simultaneously exercise our ambition, talent, and capacity for learning and contribute to society and its organizations and institutions without becoming cormorants, doing the work but never enjoying the intrinsic benefits of the work? Our parents, our schools, and our organizations all, however inadvertently, conspire against us when they focus on the development of a career, with the rest of life merely an unanticipated consequence of the career, or even when they stress the how-to's of a career, rather than the whys.

Don Juan was explicit about this in teaching Carlos Castaneda about careers in *The Fire from Within* (1984). To have a path of knowledge, a path with a heart, makes for a joyful journey, he said, and is the only conceivable way to live. We must then think carefully about our paths before we set out on them, for by the time a person discovers that his path "has no heart," the path is ready to kill him. At that point, few of us have the courage to abandon the path, lethal as it may be, because we have invested so much in it, have become so successful at it, and to choose a new path seems dangerous, even irresponsible. And so we continue dutifully, if joylessly, along. Being the natural or adopted descendants of Puritans, we remain suspicious of joy anyway and comfortable, to an extent, in our rings. It's time for all of us to consider not only slipping out of the rings we've worn willingly ourselves but also not encumbering our new young employees with rings.

I recently concluded a five-year odyssey into the workings of leadership—superleaders, people of enormous and, in some cases, exquisite achievements in the arts, athletics, and public life, as well as industry. In the course of my explorations, I discovered several things. First, true leaders lead fully integrated lives, in which their careers and their personal lives fit seamlessly and harmoniously together. Professional and private activities complement and enhance each other. Second, true leaders have never been cormorants, even for a moment. Their ambition, talent, and capacity to learn have served them, rather than enslaving them. Third, by using their ambition, talent, and capacity, these leaders have identified their true calling, as it were, and fulfilled their own genius, their visions of excellence, through the application of passion, energy, and focus.

As the leader has learned to fulfill his or her own vision, so it is at least part of the leader's job to assist employees to fulfill their own visions. This is a less altruistic process than you might think.

The cormorant is merely efficient, but the freed bird is inspired to achieve everything it is capable of doing, and there isn't a company in America that wouldn't benefit from a little less efficiency and a lot more inspiration.

To set the visions of one's employees loose isn't always easy. After all, they have been through the mill, too, and have in many cases chosen their own rings. For example, a young man may have learned early that he had a gift for numbers and therefore chosen the path of numbers, without even bothering to test his other talents. You may see in your young numbers man a flair for design, but the very idea of moving into unknown territory may seem frightening to him, so he may resist, and you may find yourself facing a difficult choice. Either you can persist, pushing him to fulfill his true talents, or you can withdraw and settle for his more commonplace skills. Real leaders, of course, persist, because they are unwilling to settle for anything less than the best—in themselves, their organization, and their employees. In this way, leaders' passion, energy, and focus beget passion, energy, and focus in their workers. Watch a great conductor or football coach in action and you will see what I mean. The members of the orchestra or the team are not dutiful but are inspired.

This has not been a good decade for American business, and at least part of the problem resides in its elevation of obedience over imagination. Ironically, the very businesses that have suffered the most, such as the auto industry, were founded by people who were far more imaginative than they were obedient. By the same token, those businesses that are flourishing now, such as the computer industry, care little for obedience but put a premium on imagination. America itself emerged out of simultaneous disobedience and vision. But in the current climate, vision is a fragile thing and needs to be nourished and developed in executives as well as employees and co-workers.

It isn't easy, of course, or without risks, which is why too many executives prefer to deal with simple day-to-day problems and settle for small wins, rather than trying to deal with the overarching problems. But, as I see it, one of the greatest threats to American business, perhaps the ultimate threat, is its narrowing of horizons, its tendency to restrict its vision and devote its principal energies to just hanging in there, denying the sense of wide-ranging possibilities, of entire worlds to conquer that used to animate American business and made it one of the wonders of the world.

This narrowing of horizons has, of course, been noticed by our young people and is reflected now in their own attitudes. More and more young people are merely ambitious, even greedy, and perfectly willing to play the cormorant. An ophthalmologist, a leader in his field, told me not long ago that the young people entering his profession scared him to death. "They care nothing for the work, only for the money. One told me that he chose the field because it meant short office hours, no emergencies, and a lot of money for a little work." I asked him how these young people had got so greedy. He said, "They grew up in a greedy world. It's all they know." We have all participated in the making of this ever-narrowing world, and it is time now that we work to unmake it, by freeing ourselves and our fellow workers, if for no other reason than that it isn't working.

As technology advances on every front, as our tools become more accomplished and more sophisticated, we are more capable than ever of realizing our visions, even our more extravagant visions. Yet the more we are able to do, the less we seem to do. We are in danger of becoming, in Thoreau's words, "the tools of our tools," mere operators rather than explorers, mechanics rather than inventors. The world doesn't need any more operators or mechanics, but it desperately needs explorers and inventors—people willing to take on the world and its problems by living up to their own visions of excellence and using their talents to the full. Again, this isn't as altruistic as it seems.

Anyone who isn't seeking fulfillment because of fear of failing or looking foolish isn't happy, any more than the cormorant is happy, however successful that person may be. As John Mason Brown once said, "The only true happiness comes from squandering yourselves for a purpose." America in general, and American business in particular, need more squanderers and fewer cormorants.

17

A Bright Future
for Complexity

Alfred North Whitehead cautioned us to "seek simplicity and then distrust it." Unfortunately, too many people seek and accept simplistic solutions for complex problems and never question them at all. As a result, the latest miracle drug has dangerous side effects, lawmakers enact bills and then discover consequences that they never imagined, manufacturers develop great new products that are more trouble than they are worth, and CEOs bring in expensive consultants who create chaos rather than order. We are so intent now on finding answers that we listen earnestly to anyone who claims to be an expert.

The fact is that there are too many predicaments, too many grievances, too many ironies, polarities, dichotomies, dualities, ambivalences, paradoxes, contradictions, confusions, complexities, and messes, and so we naturally incline toward people with answers—without even bothering to wonder what the questions, the real questions, are. But until we begin asking the right questions, we cannot possibly come up with the right answers. Rather than trying to figure out the questions, however, we accept any answer, no matter how spurious, or find a convenient villain. The airlines said that regulations were hampering them. Today, deregulation is killing them. The auto industry said that government fiats were murdering it. Today, it begs the government to kill the foreign competition. When the White House goofs, it blames the media.

Instead of seeking easy answers and scapegoats, it's time for us to grow up and start using our heads to identify the real problems and the true villains. Simplistic solutions are usually the forerunners of people who thrive on them—such as political bosses and TV ministers. Our collective incapacity to tolerate ambiguity in the face of enormously complicated problems has led us to an almost automatic acceptance of instant relief. Some of us turn to drugs, others to exotic rituals and gurus, others to very conspicuous consumption, and all of us, at one time or another, to "experts." But, sooner or later, each of us has to accept the fact that complexity is here to stay and that order begins in chaos. Blake wrote, "Without contraries, there is no progression." The instant solution almost always expunges significant options.

The poet Luis Borges must have had that in mind when he quoted from "a certain Chinese encyclopedia," which completely upends our current system of categories. He writes, "animals are divided into: a) belonging to the Emperor, b) embalmed, c) tame, d) sucking pigs, e) sirens, f) fabulous, g) stray dogs, h) included in the present classification, i) frenzied, j) innumerable, k) drawn with a very fine camelhair brush, l) et cetera, m) having just broken the water pitcher, n) that from a long way off look like flies." Borges's "Chinese encyclopedia" makes a shambles of our patterned responses, as does a really good joke or poem or gifted mentor. It tests our minds as well by challenging us to start thinking about things in a new or at least different way.

Until dull parents, teachers, or peers turn them into automatons, children have the instinctive ability to see things in new or different ways, and so do leaders. In fact, there are many resemblances between poets, children, and leaders. All are simple but never simplistic, all are full of questions and skeptical of easy answers, all trust their instincts, and all are capable of simultaneous truth and originality. Consider any true American leader, from Thomas Jefferson to Henry Ford to Martin Luther King. Each was a dreamer yet practical, an original yet totally in sync with his constituents, and each made something new. Jefferson made our Declaration of Independence, Ford gave us a vehicle that made us independent, and King gave us a dream that might have made us all free, if we had had the courage to make the dream real. Today, anyone who aspires to leadership in America must learn more about the complex roots of our various predicaments, must learn how to identify the real questions and thereby begin to come up with some workable answers.

Fifty years ago, a character in an E. B. White story said, "I predict a bright future for complexity. Have you ever considered how complicated things can get, what with one thing always leading to another?" On the off chance that you're still thinking that the current complexity will go away, here's a list of some of the current problems, chosen more or less at random:

Accelerating change
Anemic or inept managers
Balkanization of U.S. society and/or the end of consensus
Big government, big media, big corporations, big everything
Bureaucracy
Continuing hunger
Corporate scandals
Crime
Crisis of public education
Dehumanization
Eclipse of community
End of the "melting pot" hypothesis
Failure of "bigness"
Fragmentation—of life, work, ideas, solutions, world views, family
Government—city, county, state, national
Greed
Gridlock—freeway, corporate, personal

Hedonism
Hypocrisy of corporate America
Illiteracy
Legal and illegal cover-ups
Lobbyists
Media
Moral/spiritual decline and/or rise
New concepts of growth
New concepts of no growth
People unable to realize their potential, or "people are no
    damned good"
Poverty
Privacy and secrecy
Restrictions of freedom
Shift toward conservatism
Shift toward liberalism
Taxes
Technology
Third World
Twilight of the hydrocarbon era
Wall Street
Welfare
Women's movement
Work

18

Letting Virtues Shine Through

Humanity has walked on the moon, has hurled a satellite 600 million miles into space to send back telephotos of Jupiter, has conquered disease and ignorance, and has raised a remarkable number of people to a standard of living that by medieval standards is truly regal. Individuals have produced brilliant works of art that inspire and instruct us. We have, it would seem, advanced to a degree that our ancestors could not even have imagined. But they probably could not have imagined our foolishness either—our profligate waste of the earth's resources, our continuing devotion to war as a means of settling disputes, our investing billions in weapons we claim we won't use, our apparent inability to educate our young people and care humanely for the poor, the sick, and the elderly, our addictions to drugs, and, perhaps most of all, our appalling ignorance of ourselves.

It is the nature of Americans to hope. André Maurois said we were, "in a word, optimists." I am, obviously, an optimist or I wouldn't have spent my life striving to find ways for us to use ourselves better and more fully. Each of us is, in a sense, a miser who has vast resources that he or she hoards rather than spends. Even a genius uses, at most, only 80 percent of his or her potential. Few of us use even 50 percent, and, in these fast, mean times, we seem unwilling to use our best qualities at all. Our best qualities are integrity, dedication, magnanimity, humility, openness, and creativity. These, of course, are the basic ingredients of leadership, and our unwillingness to tap these qualities in ourselves explains, to a large extent, the leadership shortage.

By *integrity*, I mean standards of moral and intellectual honesty on which our conduct is based. Without integrity, we betray ourselves and others and cheapen every endeavor. It is the single quality whose absence we feel most sharply on every level of our national life. But the nation's integrity will be restored only when each of us asserts his or her own integrity. By their very existence, people of integrity lend hope to our innate conviction that we, as a people, can rise above the current moral cynicism and squalor. As Aristotle wrote in *Ethics*, "If you would understand virtue, observe the conduct of virtuous men."

Recently, the nation has hunted for the real villains of the Iran-Contra scandal and the insider trading scandal, along with the Gary Hart and Tammy and Jim Bakker debacles. Wherever we turn, we confront ourselves. This current rash of scandals is the sum of a million and one undiscovered, uncounted small cheatings, evasions, cover-ups, half-truths, and moral erosions not only in our alleged leaders but in the whole society. The slogan for these seedy times is "Everybody does it." Integrity, like charity, begins at home. Only when each of us asserts his or her own integrity will it be restored to the nation.

By *dedication*, I mean a passionate belief in something. This sort of intense and abiding commitment is the basis for great works of art, inventions, scientific discoveries, explorations, and lives. It is what makes marriages, corporations, and governments work. Indeed, absolute fidelity to someone or something makes us more fully human.

Human beings cannot live wholly and fully without giving themselves without reservation to something beyond themselves. Dedicated citizens do not simply write letters to their representatives in Congress, they involve themselves at the grass-roots level in politics and work actively for the causes they support. In the same way, they do not simply deplore the plight of the homeless but do whatever they can to alleviate their plight. For instance, a great many homeless people have gathered on the beach in Venice, California. Some people agitate for their removal—by force, if necessary—seeing them as, at least, a nuisance. Others, the dedicated citizens, press the Los Angeles City Council and county supervisors to institute measures to materially aid these people and, in the interim, supply them with clean clothing and daily hot meals. Dedicated workers—whether they sell insurance or write novels or run corporations—not only do better work, they do it joyfully.

By *magnanimity,* I mean, as the dictionary says, being "noble of mind and heart; generous in forgiving; above revenge or resentment." In the midst of the Civil War, with the fate of the Union in his hands, Abraham Lincoln called at the home of General George McClellan, found him out, and waited an hour with his secretary, John Hay. When McClellan came home and was told that Lincoln was waiting, he sent word that he had retired. Lincoln left, with Hay fuming at McClellan's insolence. Lincoln said, "I will hold McClellan's horse if he will bring us a victory." That's magnanimity. It's also akin to humility.

Magnanimous and/or humble people are notable for their self-possession. They know who they are, have healthy egos, and take more pride in what they do than in who they are. They take compliments with a grain of salt and take intelligent criticism without rancor. Such people learn from their mistakes and don't harp on the mistakes of others. They are gracious winners and losers. Tennis star John McEnroe is neither magnanimous nor humble. Albert Schweitzer and Albert Einstein were. Today, there are far more McEnroes than there are Schweitzers and Einsteins, and self-possession declines as self-importance rises. True leaders are, by definition, both magnanimous and humble.

By *openness,* I mean a willingness to try new things and hear new ideas, however bizarre, a tolerance for ambiguity and change, and a rejection of any and all preconceived prejudices, biases, and stereotypes. The open-minded person does not rank people according to race, color, religion, or occupation, does not measure ideas on the basis of their source, will eat or drink virtually anything once, including snake meat, will read unknown, uncelebrated writers, listen to his or her children's CDs, and watch performance artists doing eccentric things. Open-mindedness does not make such a person uncritical, but it does inspire him or her to be both adventurous and creative.

We seem to lose our creativity, or at least let it atrophy, as we grow up. This is too bad, as every child under ten is not only creative but original, while most adults not only are uncreative but are copies of other adults. Stand outside any urban office building in the morning and count the number of men *not* wearing the usual pinstripes or grey worsted suit with the mandatory power tie, which is, at the moment, yellow. These people make a lot of money and have a lot of responsibility, yet they lack either the creativity or the courage to choose suits that are different from all the other suits. Unfortunately, their minds are generally as conventional as their garb.

Creativity is something that we are all born with and that almost all of us manage to lose. We don't really see the world around us. We may see a flower but not the miracle of it, its intricate structure, its complete harmony, its amazing colors. To restore our creativity, we must restore our sense of wonder, to break through our own preconceptions and see everything new and fresh—as we did when we were children. This means making the familiar strange and making the strange familiar.

The more our work makes us specialists, the more we must strive to remain or become generalists in other matters, to perceive the interconnections between science, esthetics, and ethics, to avoid becoming lopsided. All of humanity's pursuits are connected, after all, and we remain ignorant of those connections at our peril. The surgeon, the CEO, the account executive, the broker all need to know as much as they can about everything if they want to understand anything. Robots and computers can do virtually everything people can do now, but they cannot be creative, which, at bottom, might be defined as thinking for yourself. Einstein once said, "The most incomprehensible thing about the universe is that it is comprehensible."

Creative people strive to comprehend as much as they can of it, to truly see, hear, and understand, to connect, and to make something worthy out of all that.

Integrity, dedication, magnanimity, humility, openness, and creativity—or, more succinctly, vision and virtue—are in all of us, however rusty or dormant they may be. Anyone who intends to lead us out of the current slough will have to exercise both.

19

Quitting on Principle

What do you do when the leader is wrong? Not just mistaken or slightly off base in his judgment, but wrong? Arnold Burns and William Weld, when faced with a situation in which they felt that U.S. Attorney General Edwin Meese was destroying the Justice Department, responded with the drama that the situation called for: They went to President Reagan, who supposedly listened "open-mouthed" as they told him what was going on. They resigned their positions as the number-two and number-three men in the Justice Department. And they went to the press.

    I first began seriously considering the question of resignation and other expressions of dissent as organizational phenomena in the spring of 1970. At that time, I had just resigned as acting executive vice-president of the State University of New York, Buffalo. As so often happens, my interest in the phenomenon grew out of unpleasant personal experience. I had resigned in protest against what I considered undue use of force on the part of the university's acting president in dealing with a series of student strikes on our campus that spring. In my case, resigning turned out to be a remarkably ineffective form of protest for many reasons, notably my decision to retain another administrative position while resigning the acting post. The distinction between the positions was clear only to other members of the administration, and the public generally interpreted my equivocal exit as a halfhearted protest. When I tried to analyze why it was ineffective, I found that my experience was hardly unique, that most large organizations, including government agencies and universities, have well-oiled mechanisms for neutralizing dissent. The individual who can force the organization into a public confrontation, as Burns and Weld and a few others have done, is rare indeed.

Of course, this is not the first time in recent history that members of the Justice Department have resigned over a principle. Attorney General Elliott Richardson and his immediate successor resigned and very publicly refused to obey President Nixon's order to fire Special Prosecutor Archibald Cox. In an act that would live to haunt him, Solicitor General Robert Bork *did* fire Cox rather than join in the resignations known as the Saturday Night Massacre. In another clear case of public protest less than a year later, President Ford's press secretary, J. F. terHorst, resigned after Ford pardoned Nixon. But even with more recent examples at hand, the Daniel Ellsberg case remains one of the most compelling. Ellsberg, you may recall, was the Rand employee who released classified material to the *New York Times*—material later known as the Pentagon Papers.

No matter how often Ellsberg reminded the public that not he but a seemingly endless war in Indochina was at issue, I always found that it was Ellsberg the man who touched the imagination. One couldn't help speculating on his personal odyssey from loyal insider to defiant outsider, from organization man to prison-risking dissident. It is the process of that change of heart that fascinates me. What interaction between person and organization produces a commitment like the younger Ellsberg's and then leads only a few years later to equally passionate rejection? How much of the Ellsberg affair is idiosyncratic, and how much reflects general principles of organizational life? After all, Ellsberg was not the first government adviser to become suspicious of the work in which he had engaged.

What was singular about Ellsberg is that he found a dramatic way to make his dissent articulate. The organizational ethic is typically so strong that even the individual who dissents and opts for the outside by resigning or otherwise dissociating him- or herself usually does so with organization-serving discretion. Ellsberg may not have broken the law, but he surely did something more daring. He broke the code. He not only spoke out, he produced documentation of his disillusionment.

The stakes are rarely as great, but many people who work in large, bureaucratic organizations find themselves in a position similar to Ellsberg's. They oppose some policy, and they quickly learn that bureaucracies do not tolerate dissent. When then? They have several options: They can capitulate. Or they can remain within the group and try to win the majority over to their own position, enduring the frustration and ambiguity that go with this option. Or they can resign. Remaining can be an excruciating experience of public loyalty and private doubt. But what of resigning? Superficially, resignation seems an easy out, but it also has its dark and conflictual side. And if resignation is the choice, the problem of how to leave, whether silently or openly voicing one's position, still remains.

These options are a universal feature of organizational life, and yet virtually nothing has been written on the dynamics of dissent in organizations, except for a now-classic book by Harvard political economist Albert O. Hirschman (1970), *Exit, Voice, and Loyalty.*

The garden-variety resignation is an innocuous act, no matter how righteously indignant the individual who tenders it. The act is made innocuous by a set of organization-serving conventions that few resignees are able (or, for a variety of personal reasons, even willing) to break. When the properly socialized dissenter resigns, he or she tiptoes out. A news release is sent to the media on the letterhead of the departing one's superior. "I today accepted with regret the resignation of Mister/Ms./Doctor Y," it reads. The pro forma statement rings pure tin in the discerning ear, but this is the accepted ritual nonetheless. One retreats under a canopy of smiles, with verbal bouquets and exchanges, however insincere, of mutual respect. The last official duty of the departing one is to keep his or her mouth shut. The rules of play require that the last word goes to those who remain inside.

The purpose served by this convention is a purely institutional one. Announcement of a resignation is usually a sign of disharmony and possibly real trouble within an organization. But without candid follow-up by the individual making the sign, it is an empty gesture. The organization reasons, usually correctly, that the muffled troublemaker will soon be forgotten. With the irritant gone, the organization pursues its chosen course, subject only to the casual and untrained scrutiny of the general public.

The striving of organizations for harmony is less a conscious program than a consequence of the structure of large organizations. Cohesiveness in such organizations results from a commonly held set of values, beliefs, norms, and attitudes, often summed up as culture. In other words, an organization can be a judgmental place in which those who do not share the common set, the common point of view, are by definition deviant, marginal outsiders.

Ironically, this pervasive emphasis on harmony does not serve organizations particularly well. Unanimity leads rather quickly to stagnation, which, in turn, invites change by nonevolutionary means. The fact that the organizational deviant, the individual who sees things differently, may be the institution's vital and only link with some new, more apt paradigm does not make the organization value that person any more. Most organizations would rather risk obsolescence than make room for the nonconformists in their midst.

This is most true when such intolerance is most suicidal; that is, when the issues involved are of major importance (or when important people have taken a very strong or a personal position). On matters such as whether to name a new product "Corvair" or "Edsel," or whether to establish a franchise in Peoria or Oshkosh, dissent is reasonably well tolerated, even welcomed, as a way of ensuring that the best of all possible alternatives is finally implemented. But when it comes to war or peace, life or death, growth or organizational stagnation, fight-

ing or withdrawing, reform or status quo—desperately important matters—dissent is typically seen as fearful. Exactly at that
time when it is most necessary to consider the possible consequences of a wide range of alternatives, a public show of consensus becomes an absolute value to be defended no matter
what the human cost.

Unanimity, or at least its public show, is so valued within
the organizational context that it often carries more weight
with an individual than his or her own conscience. Thus we
noted in the March 31, 1971, issue of the *New York Times* that
"Muskie regrets silence on war" and wishes that he had made
public as far back as 1965 his "real doubts about involvement in
the Vietnam war." Instead, he said, "he voiced his concerns privately to President Johnson." "There are two ways," he said,
"and they're both legitimate ways of trying to influence public
policy. And I can guess the tendency is, when the President is
a member of your own party and you're a senator, to try to express your doubts directly to him, in order to give him a chance
to get the benefit of your views." Muskie said he often had
done that "but wished that I'd expressed my doubts publicly at
that time." The article goes on to say that Muskie "was far less
hesitant to criticize President Nixon's conduct of the war."

In an adjoining article, the *Times* reported how Hubert
Humphrey first publicly described, to a student audience, the
pressure he had been under from President Johnson not to
speak out on the Vietnam issue. Many times during the first
month of the 1968 presidential campaign, he recalled, he had
wanted to speak out more forcefully on the Vietnam issue, only
to be dissuaded by the president. This, he said, posed a personal
dilemma. On the one side, he said, he saw his chances for winning the presidency slipping away. But, he said, he was being
warned by the president that if he sought headlines on the Vietnam issue by taking a more critical stance, he would jeopardize
the delicate negotiations then under way to bring South Vietnam and the Vietcong to the Paris negotiating table. "That's the
God's truth. . . . How would you like to be in that jam?" Humphrey asked a student.

Actually, Humphrey's "jam" is a classic one. A member

of an organization, in this case the Johnson administration, suddenly finds him- or herself opposed to his or her superior and colleagues in regard to some policy. If the policy is relatively unimportant or not yet firm, the objection may be absorbed by bargaining or compromise. If the issue at stake is actually trivial, it may simply be avoided. But if the issue is important and the dissenter adamant, the gulf begins to widen.

At first, the dissenter tries to exert all possible influence over the others, tries to bring the others around. In Albert Hirschman's compact terminology, this is the option of *voice.* Short of calling a press conference, this option can be exercised in several ways, from simply grumbling to threatening to resign. But usually the individual gives voice to his or her dissatisfaction in a series of private confrontations like those of Muskie and Humphrey with Johnson. When these fail, as they usually do, the dissenter must face the possibility of resigning (or, as Hirschman calls it, exercising the option to *exit).*

Resigning becomes a reasonable alternative as soon as voice begins to fail. The individual realizes that hours of sincere, patient argument have come to nothing, that his or her influence within the organization is waning, and so, probably, is his or her loyalty. If the individual stays on, he or she risks becoming an organizational eunuch, an individual of no influence publicly supporting a policy against his or her will, judgment, personal value system, at times even against the professional code.

As bleak as this prospect is, exit on matters of principle is still a distinctly uncommon response to basic institutional conflict. This is particularly true of American politics, despite the examples cited at the beginning of this chapter.

In a postmortem on the Johnson administration, James Reston stated that the art of resigning on principle from high government positions in the United States has almost disappeared. Anthony Eden and Duff Cooper left Neville Chamberlain's cabinet with a clear, detailed explanation of why they could no longer be identified with the policy of appeasement. Nobody did that over Vietnam. Most of those who remained during the critical period of the escalation of the war gave the president the loyalty they owed to the country. Afterward, in private life, some of them wondered whether this was really in the national interest.

What accounts for our national reluctance to resign and our willingness, when forced to take the step, to settle for a "soft exit," without clamor, without a public statement of principle, and ideally without publicity? Tremendous institutional pressures and personal rationalizations work together to dissuade the dissident from exit in favor of voice. Most of us would much rather convince the boss or top group to see "reason" than to quit. Resignation is defiant, an uncomfortable posture for most organization men (including politicians and academics). Worse, it smacks of failure, the worst of social diseases among the achievement oriented. So, instead of resigning, we reason to ourselves that the organization could go from bad to worse if we resigned. This may be the most seductive rationalization of all. Meanwhile, we have become more deeply implicated in the policy that we silently oppose, making extrication progressively more difficult.

If resignation cannot be avoided, there are selfish reasons for doing it quietly. Most resignees would like to work again. Only the producers of "60 Minutes" love a blabbermouth. Speaking out is not likely to enhance one's marketability. A negative aura haunts the visibly angry resignee, while the individual who leaves a position ostensibly to return to business, family, teaching, or research reenters the job market without any such cloud. Many resignees prefer a low profile simply because they are aware that issues change. Why undermine one's future effectiveness by making a noisy but ineffectual stand? However selfish the reasons, the organization reaps the major benefits when an individual chooses to resign quietly. A decorous exit conceals the underlying dissension that prompted the resignation in the first place. And the issue at contest is almost sure to be obscured by the speech making.

Like the Zen tea ceremony, resigning is a ritual, and woe to the person who fails to do it according to the rules. For example, when Fred Friendly resigned as president of CBS News in 1966 over the airing of Vietnam hearings, he sinned by releasing a news story *before* the chair of the board, William S.

Paley, could distribute his own release. Friendly (1967) writes in his memoir of this episode, *Due to Circumstances Beyond Our Control:*

> Around two o'clock a colleague suggested that I should have called Paley, who was in Nassau, and personally read my letter [of resignation] to him over the phone. When I called Stanton to ask him if he had read my letter to the chairman, he said that he had just done so, and that Paley wanted me to call him. When I did, Paley wanted to know only if I had released my letter; when I told him that I had, all useful communication ceased. "You volunteered to me last week that you would not make a public announcement," he said. . . . The last thing the chairman said to me was: "Well, if you hadn't put out that letter, maybe we could still have done something." I answered that my letter was "after the fact, long after."

Paley's response is explicable only if we remember that the *fact* of resignation and the *reasons* behind it are subordinated in the organizational scheme to the issue of institutional face saving. A frank resignation is regarded by the organization as an act of betrayal. (To some degree, this is, of course, an issue of personal face saving. Those in power may wish for institutional harmony in part as a protection against personal criticism.) Because a discreet resignation amounts to no protest at all, a soft exit lifts the opprobrium of organizational deviation from the resignee. When Dean Acheson bowed out as under secretary of the treasury in 1933 after a dispute with President Roosevelt over fiscal policy, his discretion was boundless, and Roosevelt was duly appreciative. Some years later, when another official left with less politesse, sending the White House a sharp criticism of the president's policies, Roosevelt returned the letter with the tart suggestion that the man ought to "ask Dean Acheson how a gentlemen resigns."

But "hard" or "soft," exit remains the option of last resort in organizational life. Remarkably, the individual who is deeply opposed to some policy often opts for public acquiescence and private frustration. Such a person may continue to voice his or her opposition to colleagues, but they are able to neutralize the protest in various ways. Thus we saw George Ball becoming the official devil's advocate of the Johnson administration. As George E. Reedy (1975) wrote in *Twilight of the Presidency*:

> During President Johnson's Administration I watched George Ball play the role of devil's advocate with respect to foreign policy. The cabinet would meet and there would be an overwhelming report from Robert McNamara, another overwhelming report from Dean Rusk, another overwhelming report from McGeorge Bundy. Then five minutes would be set aside for George Ball to deliver his dissent, and because they expected him to dissent, they automatically discounted whatever he said. This strengthened them in their own convictions because the cabinet members could quite honestly say: "We heard both sides of this issue discussed." Well, they heard it with wax in their ears. I think that the moment you appoint an official devil's advocate you solidify the position he is arguing against.

One can hardly imagine a predicament more excruciating than Ball's. Often people in such conflict with the rest of their organization simply remove themselves, if not physically then by shifting their concern from the issues to practical problems of management and implementation. They distract themselves. Townsend Hoopes (1970) suggests that this was the case with Robert McNamara. According to Hoopes, who was under secretary of the air force, there was growing evidence in the autumn of 1967 that the president and McNamara were growing further and further apart in their attitudes toward escalating the Vietnam war. Hoopes saw in McNamara the fatigue and loneliness of a man "in deep doubt" as to the course the war was taking. But, writes Hoopes:

> Owing to his own strict conception of loyalty to the President, McNamara found it officially necessary to deny all doubt and, by his silence, to discourage doubt in his professional associates and subordinates. . . . The result of McNamara's ambivalence, however, was to create a situation of dreamlike unreality for those around him. His staff meetings during this period were entirely barren affairs: a technical briefing, for example, on the growing strength of air defenses around Hanoi, but no debate on what this implied for the U.S. bombing effort, and never the slightest disclosure of what the President or the Secretary of State might consider the broad domestic and international implications to be. It was an atmosphere that worked to neutralize those who were the natural supporters of his concerns about the war.

What Hoopes describes is ethical short-circuiting. Conflict-torn McNamara busies himself with the minutiae of war planning because lists of numbers and cost estimates have a distracting if illusory moral neutrality. According to Hoopes, toward the end of McNamara's tenure, the despairing secretary stopped questioning the military and political significance of sending 206,000 more troops into Indochina and concentrated in the short time he had on the logistical problems of getting them to the port of debarkation safely and efficiently.

One sees a remarkably similar displacement of energy from moral or political concerns to managerial or technological ones in the career of Albert Speer. (I do not mean to label McNamara a fascist by literary association.) The pages of *Inside the Third Reich* reveal that Speer dealt with ambivalence brought on by intense organizational stress in a remarkably similar way. Speer did not allow his growing personal reservations about Hitler to interfere with his meticulous carrying out of administrative duties. Speer kept the Nazi war machine running in high gear and increasingly productive until 1945. As Eugene Davidson writes, "A man like Speer, working with blueprints, ordering vast projects, is likely to exhaust himself in manipulation, in transforming the outer world, in carrying out production goals with all the means at hand."

Whether such activity exhausts an individual to the point of moral numbness is questionable, but certainly the nature of the large organization makes it possible for a McNamara or an Albert Speer or an Ellsberg (while at Rand), for that matter, to work toward an ultimately immoral end without an immediate sense of personal responsibility or guilt. Organizations are by definition systems of increased differentiation and specialization, and thus the morality of the organization is the morality of segmented acts. As Charles Reich (1970) wrote in *The Greening of America*, "A scientist who is doing his specialized duty to further research and knowledge develops a substance called napalm. Another specialist makes policy in the field of our nation's foreign affairs. A third is concerned with the most modern weaponry. A fourth manufactures what the defense authorities require. A fifth drops napalm from an airplane where he is told to do so." In this segmented environment, any one individual can easily develop tunnel vision, concentrating on the task at hand, completing the task with a sense of accomplishment, however sinister the collective result of all these individual jobs well done. This segmented structure, characteristic of all large organizations, encourages indifference and evasion of responsibility. A benefit of membership in such an organization is insurance against the smell of burning flesh. Speer, for example, still does not seem particularly troubled by the horrors of slave labor in his wartime munitions plants even when making his unique public confession.

Speer reports that it never occurred to him to resign, even though he was aware of what his loss would do to hasten the end of Hitler's regime. Faced with a much more subtle and complex situation, McNamara seriously considered resigning, according to Hoopes. But that he did not do so in 1967 when his doubts were so oppressive is remarkable. Hoopes provides a fascinating clue to McNamara's reluctance to resign or even to voice his uneasiness in any except the most private audiences with the president. In the following short portrait by Hoopes (1970), we see McNamara wrestling with an ingrained organizational ethic stronger than his own intelligence and instinct:

> Accurately regarded by the press as the one moderate member of the inner circle, he continued to give full public support to the Administration's policy, including specific endorsement of successive manpower infusions and progressively wider and heavier bombing efforts. Inside the Pentagon he seemed to discourage dissent among his staff associates by the simple tactic of being unreceptive to it; he observed, moreover, so strict a sense of privacy in his relationship with the President that he found it virtually impossible to report even to key subordinates what he was telling the President or what the President was saying and thinking. . . .
>
> All of this seemed to reflect a well-developed philosophy of executive management relationship, derived from his years in industry; its essence was the belief that a busy, overworked chairman of the board should be spared the burden of public differences among his senior vice-presidents. Within such a framework, he could argue the case for moderation with the President—privately, selectively, and intermittently. But the unspoken corollary seemed to be that, whether or not his counsel of moderation were followed, there could arise no issue or difference with President Johnson sufficient to require his resignation—whether to enlighten public opinion or avoid personal stultification. It was this corollary that seemed of doubtful applicability to the problems and obligations of public office. *McNamara gave evidence that he had ruled out resignation because he believed that the situation would grow worse if he left the field to Rusk, Ros-*

*tow, and the Joint Chiefs. But also because the idea
ran so strongly against the grain of his tempera-
ment and his considered philosophy of organizational effectiveness* [italics mine].

Does this mean that McNamara would not resign because
quitting violated some personal notion of honor? Or does it
mean that he believed that dissent and "organizational effectiveness" are negatively correlated? I suspect that the latter is closer
to the truth. Like any other corporation president, McNamara
was raised on organizational folklore. One of the central myths
is that the show of unanimity is always desirable. That this belief is false and even dangerous does not limit its currency.

Yes, there are times when discretion is required. Clearly,
organizations should not constantly fight in public. But what is
gained by forbidding at all costs and at all times any emotional
give-and-take between colleagues? Why must a person who has
an honest difference of opinion with the organizational powers
be silenced or domesticated or driven out so that the public can
continue to believe—falsely—that organizational life is without
strife? And yet organizations continue to assume the most con-
trived postures in order to maintain the illusion of harmony—
postures such as lying to the public.

Our inability to transcend the dangerous notion that we
don't wash our dirty linen in public verges on the schizophrenic.
It implies not only that dissent is bad but that our public institutions, such as governments, are made up not of human beings
but of saints who never engage in such vulgar and offensive activities. Thus, government strives to be regarded as a hallowed
shrine where, as George Reedy (1975) reports in *Twilight of the
Presidency* about his experience as White House press secretary
under President Johnson, "the meanest lust for power can be
sanctified and the dullest wit greeted with reverential awe."

In fact, organizations, including governments, are vulgar,
sweaty, plebeian; if they are to be viable, they must create an institutional environment where a fool can be called a fool and all
actions and motivations are duly and closely scrutinized for the
inevitable human flaws and failures. In a democracy, meanness,

dullness, and corruption are always amply represented. They are not entitled to protection from the same rude challenges that such qualities must face in the "real" world. When banal politeness is assigned a higher value than accountability or truthfulness, the result is an Orwellian world where the symbols of speech are manipulated to create false realities.

"Loyalty" is often given as a reason or pretext for muffling dissent. A variation on this is the claim that candor "gives comfort to the enemy." Ellsberg's national loyalty was repeatedly questioned in connection with his release of the so-called Pentagon Papers. In the first three installments of the documents as run in the *New York Times*, practically nothing that wasn't well known was revealed. There were a few details, an interesting admission or two, but basically nothing that had not come to light earlier in other, less controversial articles and books on the Indochina war. But government officials trying to suppress the publication of the classified material chose to make much of the "foreign consequences" of its release. "You may rest assured," a government official was quoted as saying by the *Buffalo Evening News*, "that no one is reading this series any more closely than the Soviet Embassy."

All the foregoing pressures against registering dissent can be subsumed under the clumsy label of "loyalty." In fact, they represent much more subtle personal and organizational factors, including deep-rooted psychological dependence, authority problems, simple ambition, co-optive mechanisms (the "devil's advocacy" technique), pressure to be a member of the club and fear of being outside looking in, adherence to the myth that gentlemen settle their differences amicably and privately, fear of disloyalty in the form of giving comfort to "the enemy," and, very often, that powerful Prospero aspiration: the conviction that one's own "reasonable" efforts will keep things from going from bad to worse.

There is a further broad cultural factor that must be considered before the other defenses against exit can be understood. It simply doesn't make sense for a man as intelligent and analytically sophisticated as Robert McNamara to delude himself that he couldn't quit because "duty called." Duty to whom?

Not to his own principles. Nor, as he saw it, to the nation's welfare. McNamara's real loyalty was to the code of the "organizational society" in which most of us live out our entire active careers.

More than 90 percent of the employed population of this country works in formal organizations. Status, position, a sense of competence and accomplishment are all achieved in our culture through belonging to these institutions. What you *do* determines, to a large extent, what you *are*. "My son, the doctor" is not only the punch line of a thousand Jewish jokes. It is a neat formulation of a significant fact about our culture. Identification with a profession or other organization is a real-life passport to identity, to selfhood, to self-esteem. You are what you do, and work in our society (as in all other industrialized societies) is done in large, complex, bureaucratic structures. If one leaves the organization, particularly with protest, one is nowhere, like a character in a Beckett play—without role, without the props of office, without ambience or setting.

In fact, a few more resignations would be good for individual consciences and good for the country. Looking back, veteran diplomat Robert Murphy could recall only one occasion when he thought he should have resigned. The single instance was the Berlin Blockade of 1948–49, which he thought the United States should have challenged more vigorously. "My resignation almost certainly would not have affected events," he wrote in regret, "but if I had resigned, I would feel better today about my own part in that episode." The *Time* magazine article goes on to say: "In the long run, the country would probably feel better, too, if a few more people were ready to quit for their convictions. It might be a little unsettling. But it could have a tonic effect on American politics, for it would give people the assurance that men who stay truly believe in what they are doing."

My own resignation was a turning point. The decision represented the first time in many years of organizational life that I had been able to say, "No, I cannot allow myself to be identified with this particular policy," the first time I had risked being an outsider rather than trying to work patiently within the system for change. Many factors entered into the decision, but in the last analysis, my reason for resigning was an intensely personal one. I did not want to say, a month or two months after the police came onto the campus, "Well, I was against that move at the time." I think it is important for everyone in a decision-making position in any of our institutions to speak out. And if we find it impossible to continue as administrators because we are at total and continuous odds with institutional policy, then I think we must quit and go out shouting. The alternative is petit Eichmannism, and that is too high a price.

20

Canceling
the Doppelgänger Effect

One of the most striking things about the Iran-Contra hearings was how much all the alleged conspirators resembled one another in manner, posture, and speech. All seemed cast from the same mold—clean-cut, trim, conventional, full of humorless purposefulness, and empty of any moral sensibilities. In these ways, they resembled their commander in chief, as if they were all doppelgängers, ghostly doubles.

This doppelgänger phenomenon is by no means an accident and by no means confined to the White House. If spy cameras zoomed in on the headquarters of any large bureaucracy—in either the public or the private sector—they would see the effect repeated endlessly, because by and large people tend to select people to work with them who are cut from the same goods. What's worse, if the cameras zoomed in on any watering hole in any more or less affluent section of any city or suburb in America, they would find dozens of look-alikes.

As a graduate student, I did a study that showed that many chiefs tended to choose assistants who resembled them not only in ideas and attitudes but in height, stature, and dress.

Subsequently, I learned that one corporation's campus recruiters were required to note whether prospective employees "look like us."

The desire for a congenial and closely knit management group is quite human and even understandable. The sheer size of organizations makes it impossible for the top people to verify their own information, analyze their own problems, and decide whom they should spend their time with. They have to rely on their assistants to double for them in certain instances, and so, to a degree, those assistants should be of kindred minds and compatible natures. Assistants are the inevitable products of big business and are indispensable, but since they control access to their boss, choosing both the material and people the boss will see, they control the boss to an extent. There are two problems inherent in the system. First, things the boss needs to know and people the boss needs to see may be kept from him or her by overzealous assistants—either out of eagerness to protect the boss or out of simple ignorance. Second, they may, in the same spirit, exercise more authority than they have. This was certainly the case with North, Poindexter, and company.

Operating on the assumption that Reagan wanted them to aid the Contras, they broke a number of laws, lied, even deliberately shredded evidence, and, by their own lights, "protected" him by not telling him what they were doing. Rather than protecting him, they did more damage to their president than all his avowed enemies had been able to do. Ironically, Reagan, who managed to sail through six years in the White House without a mark on him, was finally knocked down by some of his most ardent supporters. Thanks to them, his popularity with the public declined, as did his ability to control Congress.

The White House bureaucracy has dramatically increased in size, is characterized by specialization and divisions of labor and responsibilities, and has an intricate chain of command and hierarchy. Further, White House functionaries actually compete with executive departments for power. During the Nixon administration and again during the Reagan presidency, White House insiders looked on the State and Defense Departments more as adversaries than as allies.

Franklin Roosevelt had three authorized assistants. Several thousand people assist Reagan, and even the divisions have divisions. Reagan now has a press secretary and a director of communications. There are additional ironies. Reagan, who campaigned against big government, had the biggest staff in the history of the White House and, with the exception of Nixon's, the most inept.

Reagan's problems were compounded by the fact that he relied heavily on his aides. He's not much of a reader, and, according to the late chief of the CIA William Casey, he doesn't like to work very hard, and so, more than any of his predecessors, he counted on his staff supplying him with everything he needed to know. His staff failed in this regard—judging by the president's numerous press conference lapses, along with the Iran-Contra scandal.

The one thing a president—whether of the United States, a corporation, or a university—needs above all is the truth, all of it, all the time, and it is the one thing a president is least likely to get from his assistants, if they are cut from the same cloth. Pierre du Pont once wrote, "One cannot expect to know what will happen, one can only consider himself fortunate if he can learn what has happened." His performance in press conferences suggests that Reagan was frequently in the dark as to what had happened.

I was myself a president for six years, president of the University of Cincinnati, and I was blessed with a staff of dedicated, honest, and intelligent men and women, with whom I had to endlessly struggle for the whole truth and nothing but the truth. When I finally pried whatever it was I needed to know out of them, they would say things like "Well, I didn't want to bother you," or "I didn't want to call you wrong in front of other people," or "I didn't want to burden you," or "I thought you were making a mistake, but I didn't want to argue with you." To paraphrase the old saw, with assistants like these, who needs enemies? I believed, during my Cincinnati tenure, that the buck indeed stopped in my office, but I was lucky to be able to find the buck, much less learn where it had stopped outside my office, and why.

Obviously, then, the top people have to surround themselves with people who can, first, recognize the truth when they see it and, second, convey it to them, whether they want to hear it or not.

In her book on China, Barbara Tuchman (1972) reports that Mao Tse-tung wanted very much to meet with President Roosevelt. On the basis of very biased information from Ambassador Pat Hurley, Roosevelt canceled the meeting. If Roosevelt had been told the truth by Hurley, he would surely have met with Mao, and the course of world history might well have been significantly altered and many disasters averted. For one thing, World War II would certainly have played itself out differently in the Pacific theater, and, for another, the Vietnam War might never have taken place at all.

In the same way, corporate CEOs are often prevented from meeting with people because their assistants make snap judgments. Imagine what might have happened if Albert Einstein, in his usual sweatshirt and sneakers, had turned up at the White House to see President Roosevelt and encountered a 1930s version of Robert Haldeman, Nixon's majordomo. Einstein not only would not have been allowed in, he would probably have been jailed as a "suspicious character."

In order to ensure that they have access to the people and things they need to know, presidents of organizations, as well as the president of the United States, should institute some simple rules:

1. Their key assistants should be rotated every two years to ensure less arrogance, more humility, and continuing openness.

2. At least some and preferably all of their assistants should have had sufficient contact with their general constituency so that they understand both the obligations and the limits of power.

3. They should run, not walk, away from the doppelgänger effect. However comforting loyalty and congeniality are, they are not sufficient. Assistants should be as diverse in viewpoint and background as possible.

4. They should read at least one daily newspaper and not rely exclusively on staff summaries for their information. Any-

one who hears only what he or she wants to hear and finds only what he or she wants to find will find him- or herself in trouble.

5. Finally, they must not rely exclusively on their intimates for information. Anyone who is in charge of an organization must be accessible to its members and its constituents. When an old woman accosted the Roman emperor Hadrian, he brushed her aside, saying that he was too busy. She replied, "Then you're too busy to be emperor," whereupon he stopped and heard her out. The president who only talks and never listens will soon have nothing to say to anyone. E. M. Forster wrote, "Only connect." And that, after all, is any CEO's primary responsibility.

It is the excessive zeal, the concealments, the arrogances and half-truths of thousands of faceless doppelgängers in hundreds of organizations—from the White House to the corner hardware store—that set off troubles. The truth may hurt, but it doesn't kill anyone—except in countries, such as Nazi Germany, where everything was turned inside out and upside down.

Then there are all those other doppelgängers—the Yuppies who look alike, dress alike, think alike, and think mostly about acquiring more money and more things. Fundamentally in it for themselves, incapable of continuing loyalty to people, causes, or organizations, they have no interest in honesty or truth, either. Unable to lead, unwilling to follow, they merely copy, but their models are as bogus as they are, and as crass. These are the hollow people, the empty suits who have mastered the art of taking without ever giving, which may be why so many of them seem to wind up in jail. The presence of these moral zombies in our midst is the most obvious manifestation of our decline into anarchy. So let us be angry at the state of the union, and let us begin to connect.

21

Leader Power That No One Has

The conspicuous absence of real leadership in the world reminds me of the Frenchman who was bowled over and nearly trampled by a noisy, unruly mob. As he stood up, he saw a small, meek man who was frantically chasing the mob, and called out, "Don't follow those people." The little man yelled back, "I have to follow them. I'm their leader."

People without leadership, leaders who follow. The more we lack leadership, the more we hunger for it. Bewildered, we wander through a world that seems to have become morally dead, where everything, including the government, seems up for sale, and where, looking for the real villains, we confront ourselves everywhere.

Thomas Wolfe wrote, "Each of us is the sum of all the things he has not counted." And the thing we have come to call Irangate is the sum of a thousand smaller, unknown Irangates. Every White House functionary who failed to tell the boss the things he knew his boss would not really want to know, lest he be, at least, "accountable," has his counterpart in a thousand other bureaucracies—including universities and corporations. Irangate, the Wall Street insider trading scandal, the transgressions of Jim and Tammy Bakker—these were not isolate but the sums of all the things we have not counted, the betrayal of basic principles at the hands of all the men and women who wield the power in our society. In the unforgettable words of cartoonist Walt Kelly, "We have met the enemy—and he is us."

If we have no worthy leaders, it is our fault, but there are other elements in the problem, too. Modern humanity is drowning in information. As Robert Stone put it, "There is more information available than there are things to know." J. Robert Oppenheimer once waggishly estimated that if new information continued to accumulate at its then-present rate, the *Physical Review*, the physicists' leading journal, would weigh more than the earth by the year 2000. Getting, handling, and interpreting information are now the dominant business of our whole economy, so when the copier breaks down, everything breaks down.

But we worship this information and are dazzled by it more than we use it, and it is often more impressive for its sheer bulk than for its real value. We have more information now than we can use, and less knowledge and understanding than we need. Indeed, we seem to collect information because we have the ability to do so, but we are so busy collecting it that we haven't devised means of using it. The true measure of any society is not what it knows but what it does with what it knows.

And, in fact, though we live in the Age of Information, most of us actually know less than our predecessors, because our schools and colleges, the primary information funnels, have deteriorated. A discouraging number of high school graduates are functional illiterates, and anyone who has recently overheard teenagers in conversation knows that English is a dying language. It is not their slang I deplore, or even their apparent affection for four-letter words, but rather the endless *likes* and *you knows*.

God knows there is a glut of information, but—outside the sciences—does it add up to more knowledge or understanding? I think not. Otherwise, novels and poetry, painting and sculpture, theater and music would be better. The arts are, in a sense, the barometer of our understanding. This glut complicates national life but does not improve it, and will not until leaders emerge who can make sense of it.

Second, as the world has divided into factions, so has America, and so consensus is harder and harder to come by. Each faction marches stubbornly to its own drummer, has its own priorities and agenda, and has nothing in common with any other faction—except the unbridled desire to triumph over all the others. The Peruvians call this *arribismo.* It means, "You've got yours, Jack, and now I'm going to get mine." It means "making it," carried to the nth power. This fragmentation and fracturing of the common accord occurred for good reason, because, in America, those on top have traditionally tried to keep everyone else down, but it makes leadership a chancy undertaking at any level. Along with internal erosion and loss of consensus have come the loss of community and civility and, for leaders, tough new challenges.

Along with these fundamental alterations in the social order have come alterations in the nature of work and the components of our economy. Today, services of all kinds, including education, account for a larger proportion of the gross national product than manufacturing does, and the fastest growing services are those provided by state and county governments, including health and welfare services, along with theme parks and fast foods.

Union demands no longer focus as much on bread-and-butter issues as on more amorphous matters, such as the climate of work, guaranteed continuing employment, benefits, and retirement plans. People insist on such guarantees when they lose faith in institutions and leaders. When everything is in flux, people grab onto whatever they can find.

It is both an irony and a paradox that precisely at the time when trust in and credibility of leaders are lowest, when people are both angry and cynical, the nation most needs leaders, people who can transcend the vacuum. Unless new leaders emerge, it seems to me that our society is in grave danger. Anarchy unabated leads inevitably to the proverbial man on horseback—or in a tank. Given this, what are the requirements, the skills, the competencies that we should seek in a leader—or that a leader should attempt to develop?

Today, there's no such thing as an archetypal or ideal

leader. Leadership is at least as much an art as a science, and the key is the people themselves, their ability to know their strengths and skills and to develop them to the hilt. Since the day has long since passed when one man, such as the first Henry Ford, could run an entire organization by himself, a leader must create a kind of executive constellation to assist him or her, and thereby multiply executive power through a realistic allocation of functions and responsibilities. But these key assistants must not, as I said earlier, mirror or shield the leader, but rather must augment him or her. This constellation must be structured to supply the leader not only with the needed services but also with the needed information, and it must have a built-in means to question, challenge, and generally test the leader's assumptions.

The bigger any bureaucracy becomes, the more it is apt to yield to a kind of incestuous relationship with itself, with middle management devoting its time to justifying its existence to itself and losing touch with the outside world. In these fractious times, organizations are particularly susceptible to a kind of siege mentality, in which the "it's us against them" attitude flourishes. During the controversy over Reagan's demands for additional aid to the Contras and his nomination of Robert Bork to the Supreme Court, he personified this siege mentality when he boasted that the Senate would reject the Bork nomination over his dead body and claimed that the Contras would have U.S. support as long as there was breath in his body. Such childish rhetoric demonstrated not Reagan's strengths but his weaknesses, as did his statement that if the Senate had the temerity to reject Bork, he would nominate someone they disliked just as much.

The emperor was finally naked, but no one in the White House had the wisdom or guts to tell him so, and, as a result, he wandered farther and farther from the point. The Reagan White House oversaw a skyrocketing deficit, an escalation of bellicosity toward everyone beyond the Rose Garden, and, simultaneously, a drastic ethical decline. Record numbers of Reaganites have faced or are facing criminal and civil charges. Obviously, along with many citizens, Reagan's own aides took his advocacy of greed very seriously. If it is a true leader's task to create not only a climate of ethical probity but a climate that encourages people to learn and grow, prizes their contributions, and cherishes their independence and autonomy, then Reagan flunked on all counts, and so does nearly everyone else who currently claims to be a leader.

22

Avoiding Disaster
During Periods of Change

I have advised numerous institutions, organizations, and corporations on the mechanics of change. As a teacher, provost, and university president, I have participated in, designed, led, and even ordered change. Constant as change has been in this century, vital as it is now, it is still hard to effect, because the sociology of institutions (any groups of two or more members) is fundamentally antichange. Here, then, are ten ways to avoid disaster during periods of change, which, of course, now means any time, all the time—except in those organizations that are dying or dead.

    1. Recruit with scrupulous honesty. Enthusiasm or plain need often inspires recruiters to transmogrify visible and real drawbacks and make them reappear as exhilarating challenges. Falsely bright pictures are painted of what is to come. Packages are sweetened even when the recruiter is trying to be balanced and fair. Recruiting is, after all, a kind of courtship ritual. The suitor displays his or her assets and masks his or her defects. The recruit, flattered by the attention and the promises, does not examine the proposal thoughtfully. He or she looks forward

to opportunities to be truly creative and imaginative and to support from the top. Inadvertently, the recruiter has cooked up the classic recipe for revolution as suggested by Aaron Wildavsky: "Promise a lot; deliver a little. Teach people to believe they will be much better off, but let there be no dramatic improvement. Try a variety of small programs but marginal in impact and severely underfinanced. Avoid any attempted solution remotely comparable in size to the dimensions of the problem you're trying to solve." When expectations are too high and promises too grand, disillusionment is inevitable. The disparity between vision and reality becomes intolerable.

2. Guard against the crazies. Innovation is seductive. It attracts interesting people. It also attracts people who will distort your ideas into something monstrous. You will then be identified with the monster and be forced to spend precious energy combating it. A change-oriented administrator should be damned sure that the people he or she recruits are change agents but not agitators. It is difficult sometimes to tell the difference between the innovators and the crazies. Eccentricities and idiosyncrasies in change agents are often useful and valuable. Neurosis isn't.

3. Build support among like-minded people, whether or not you recruited them. Change-oriented administrators are particularly prone to act as though the organization came into being the day they arrived. This is a delusion, a fantasy of omnipotence. There are no clean slates in established organizations. A new CEO can't play Noah and build the world anew with a handpicked crew of his or her own. Rhetoric about new starts is frightening to those who sense that this new beginning is the end of their careers. There can be no change without history and continuity. In addition, some of the old hands have, besides knowledge and experience, real creativity. A clean sweep, then, is often a waste of resources.

4. Plan for change from a solid conceptual base. Have a clear understanding of how to change as well as what to change. Planning changes is always easier than implementing them. A statement of goals is not a program. Any reorganization requires coherence and forcefulness, along with functional mechanisms

for change. If change is to be permanent, it must be gradual. As they say, Rome wasn't built in a day. An incremental-reform model can be successfully utilized by drawing on a rotating nucleus of people who continually read the data provided by the organization and the society in which it operates for clues that it's time to adapt. Such people must not be faddists but must be hypersensitive to ideas whose hour has come. They also know when ideas are antithetical to the organization's purposes and values and when they will enhance and strengthen the organization. It's difficult to structure such critical nuclei, but organizations cannot be assured of continued self-renewal without them.

5. Don't settle for rhetorical change. Significant change cannot simply be decreed. Any organization has two structures: one on paper and another that consists of a complex set of intramural relationships. A good administrator understands the relationships and creates a good fit between them and any planned alterations. An administrator who gets caught up in his or her own rhetoric almost inevitably neglects the demanding task of maintaining established constituencies and building new ones.

6. Don't allow those who are opposed to change to appropriate basic issues. The successful revolutionary always makes sure that respectable people are not afraid of what is to come. In the same way, the successful change agent makes sure that the old guard isn't frightened at the prospect of change. The moment such people get scared is the moment they begin to fight dirty. They not only have some built-in clout, they have tradition and history on their side, or so they will claim.

7. Know the territory. The successful administrator learns everything there is to know about his or her organization and about its locale, which often means mastering the politics of local chauvinism, along with an intelligent public relations program. In Southern California, for example, big developers are constantly being blindsided by neighborhood groups because they have not bothered to acquaint the groups with themselves and their plans. The neighborhood groups often triumph, too, forcing big changes in the planned development or even its can-

cellation. They know their rights and they know the law, and the developers haven't made the effort to know them.

8. Appreciate environmental factors. No matter how laudable or profitable or imaginative, a change that increases discomfort in the organization is probably doomed. For example, adding a sophisticated new computer system is probably a good thing, but it can instantly be seen as a bad thing if it results in overcrowded offices. An administrator who plans such a change should arrange to accommodate before proceeding.

9. Avoid future shock. When an administrator becomes too involved in planning, in the next step, in the future, he or she frequently forgets the past and neglects the present. As a result, before the plan goes into effect, employees are probably already opposed to it. They, after all, have to function in the here and now, and if their boss's eye is always on tomorrow, he or she is not giving them the attention and support they need. Furthermore, when an organization focuses too much on a vision of future greatness, everyone is bound to be disillusioned with the reality. Greatness doesn't just happen. It proceeds out of a well-made organization. And one problem with planning for the future is that there are no objective criteria against which to measure alternative solutions. There isn't even a current reality against which to test them. As a result, a planner is bound to generate future shock along with valid ideas, and since there's no surefire way to separate the two, he or she should proceed very carefully.

10. Remember that change is most successful when those who are affected are involved in the planning. This is a platitude of planning theory, but it is as true as it is trite. Nothing makes people resist new ideas or approaches more adamantly than their belief that change is being imposed on them.

The problems connected with innovation and change are common to every modern bureaucracy. University, government, and corporation all respond similarly to challenge and to crisis, with much the same explicit or implicit codes, punctilios, and mystiques. Means must be found to stimulate the pursuit of truth—that is, the true nature of the organization's problems—in an open and democratic way. This calls for classic means: an examined life, a spirit of inquiry and genuine experimentation, a life based on discovering new realities, taking risks, suffering occasional defeats, and not fearing the surprises of the future. In other words, the model for truly innovative organizations in an era of constant change is the scientific model. As scientists seek and discover truths, so organizations must seek and discover their own truths—that carefully, that thoroughly, that honestly, that imaginatively, and that courageously.

23

Dealing with
the Way Things Are

The great leaders are gone and, with them, our dreams. Everything is subject to change now. Peter Drucker recently said:

> We are witnessing what may be the death of the large company. . . . The flagships of the last 40 years, institutions like General Motors, ITT and Du Pont, have basically outlived their usefulness. . . . I think they're past their peaks. There's very little flexibility there, very little creativity. . . . There are a lot of tasks for which you need bigness, yes, but in a society with institutions of only one size—and it's a large size—in a time of transition and change, you lack something vital: the ability to experiment, the ability to fail without disastrous consequences. You know, elephants don't do well in confined spaces. Their ability to wriggle through a hole in the wall is very small. You'd be better to be a rat. . . . There are no greater failures than our present business school graduates, outside of the

152

narrowest financial sphere. The Harvard Business
School graduates are abysmal failures, because the
Business School assumes, for example, an elite,
homogenous America, and we're the most diversi-
fied country in the world. . . . The model organization of tomorrow is the symphony orchestra. Have
you ever witnessed the performance of a late Mahler symphony with 1000 people on stage? Now if
you tried our normal organization, you'd have the
chief executive conductor, six chief operating conductors, and about 22 department conductors. Instead of which you'll have one conductor only.

A few years ago, Adam Smith said, "We have decades in
which the values of the business society are paramount, in
which getting and spending are very important, and in which
money is taken for granted as the accepted yardstick. And we
have times in which public purpose surpasses private interest as
the accepted goal . . . the Reagan years will be remembered as
money-value years. The values of the fast track will be with us
awhile longer, but not forever." One hundred and fifty years
ago, Alexis de Tocqueville wrote, "Americans acquire the habit
of always considering themselves as standing alone, and they are
apt to imagine their whole destiny is in their hands. Thus not
only does democracy make every man forget his ancestors, but
it hides his descendants and separates his contemporaries from
him; it throws him back upon himself alone, and threatens in
the end to confine him entirely within the solitude of his own
heart."

Traditional structures are changing, the current greedi-
ness will subside, but we the people stand pat. In such circumstances, people in positions of authority are, at best, agents of
adjustment, striving to face things as they are and prepare for
things as they will be. America is in all kinds of trouble—from
Wall Street to Main Street. America used to lead the world in research and development, manufacturing, and marketing. Though
we continue to lead in R&D, Japan and Germany have taken
the lead in manufacturing and marketing. Currently, America's

hottest consumer item is the VCR. Fifty percent of all VCRs made are sold here; yet the VCRs sold in the United States are manufactured in Japan and Korea. Why? Perhaps because we've lost the ability to work together—even for profit. Teamwork is, after all, antithetical to our current mode, but our inability to work together, to collaborate and cooperate, is undermining America.

People in positions of authority must be alert, curious, impatient, brave, steadfast, truthful, and in focus; they must not only know what they see but say what they see. Gandhi said, "We must be the change we wish to see in the world." Thus, if people in authority believe that competence and conscience must be restored, then they must demonstrate both.

There are no easy answers, no quick fixes, no formulas. It's time to face facts, lest we all follow Boesky, North, Hart, and the Bakkers into the abyss. We are not supermen. We cannot remake the world to suit us. It's not some mere trick of fate that the high and the mighty are tumbling off their pedestals in record numbers. It is rather the inevitable result of ambition outstripping competence and conscience. Whatever the question, competence and conscience are part of the answer, and unless we accept that fundamental fact, we'll all, sooner or later, fall down.

People in authority must develop the vision and authority to call the shots. There are always risks in taking the initiative, but there are greater risks now in waiting for sure things, especially since there are very few sure things in the current volatile climate. At the same time, the people have to admit their need for leadership, for vision, for dreams.

People in authority must do more than tinker with the machinery and flex their muscles. They must have an entrepreneurial vision, a sense of perspective, along with the time and inclination to raise the fundamental questions and identify the forces that are at work on both specific organizations and society in general. Such tasks require not only imagination but a real sense of continuity so that, to paraphrase Shelley, one can see the present in the past and the future in the present, clarify problems rather than exploit them, and define issues, not exacerbate them. In this way, one can elevate problems, questions, and issues into comprehensible choices for one's constituents.

To some extent, people in authority must be educators. Our great political leaders have always tried to educate the people by transforming their messy existential groaning into understandable issues. The chieftain who responds to a drought by attacking the lack of rainfall will inspire no confidence at all. Instead of merely labeling problems—for example, "the economy"—people in authority must analyze them and offer clear alternatives. The politician who says that unemployment is deplorable tells us nothing.

People in authority must be social architects, studying and shaping what we call "the culture of work," examining the values and norms of organizations and the ways they are transmitted to the individual, and, wherever necessary, altering them. Whatever his or her goals, the person in authority must create means that will facilitate understanding and encourage participation. This means, of course, that that person's goals must be in sync with the needs and aspirations of his or her followers. Trust, especially today, does not come easily, and it is never given but must be earned. CEOs who believe that trust comes automatically, along with the perks, salary, and power, are in for some rude surprises. They must know, understand, and permit themselves to be influenced by the people they presume to lead; otherwise, their plans, however fine, will be subverted.

An organization's culture dictates the kinds of mechanisms that are needed to resolve conflicts and determines how costly, humane, fair, and reasonable the outcomes will be. A new CEO, then, must devote him- or herself immediately to understanding the culture and, where necessary, adjusting or altering it to suit his or her goals. NBC's Robert Wright's first mistake was in assuming that NBC worked like GE. The smart CEO also banishes the sort of zero-sum mentality that insists on absolute winners and absolute losers in favor of a climate of hope and reconciliation.

Any culture—national, bureaucratic, or organizational—emerges out of its particular history, geography, technology, and philosophy. No two are alike. Some are essentially relaxed and coherent. Others are frenzied and chronically cranky. One businessman I know swears that he can "read" an organization's culture by talking with any base-line employee—a clerk or assembly-line worker—as well as measuring the character and posture of its top person. I decided to test his theory. Knowing that I was scheduled to have dinner with the CEO of a major department store chain, I went to one of his stores and bought a tie. On the basis of my acrimonious encounter with a sales clerk who managed to be both petulant and inefficient, I concluded that the man in charge was insecure, difficult, and arrogant, and I was right on all counts. Each employee is, to a remarkable extent, the organization in miniature. The top person must understand all this and be something of a social anthropologist in addition to being an architect, in order to know, maintain, and even alter the culture.

If people of authority are to succeed, they must know themselves and listen to themselves, integrating their ideals and actions but being able, at the same time, to tolerate the gap between the desirable and the necessary as they work to close it. They must know how to not merely listen but hear, not merely look but see, to play as hard as they work, and to live with ambiguity and inconsistency. The ultimate test of anyone in authority is whether he or she can successfully ride and direct the tides of change and, in doing so, grow stronger. As Sophocles said, "It is hard to learn the mind of any mortal, or the heart, till he be tried in chief authority. Power shows the man" (*Antigone*). And the thoughtful, imaginative, and effective use of power is what separates leaders from people in authority.

Leadership is more practice than theory, then, and is practiced in the real world, not a laboratory. Aside from his or her personal and occasionally private life, the leader's world is divided into two camps: people who answer to him or her and people he or she answers to.

The typical organization of today is big or complex or both and is surrounded by an active environment that in the last several decades has become increasingly influential and dominant in the making of organizational policy. Leaders' decisions are inevitably influenced by both camps. The people they are responsible for now, as a matter of course, demand more from them—on both traditional questions, such as conditions in the workplace, and new questions, such as maternity leaves. The people they are responsible to—from boards and shareholders to local, state, and federal governments to customers or constituents—have never been more vocal and more trigger-happy. Then, of course, there are the omnipresent, omnivorous media, which are used by adversaries more and more frequently and which are themselves sometimes adversaries. With the advent of TV, the media's influence and impact multiplied radically, and, since the 1960s, the media have seen themselves as watchdogs. This not only traps leaders in a kind of constant spotlight but requires them to do much of their work in public.

Then, too, because people are more interested in business and money, there has been a literal explosion in business coverage—daily TV and radio programs, dozens of publications, ranging from *Forbes* and *Fortune* to Xeroxed newsletters. Business-oriented media have limited focus but apparently unlimited license to cover the field, and so leaders are required to some extent to play to the media while avoiding playing for them.

In addition to setting goals and policies to achieve those goals, inspiring followers to work toward those goals, and creating an encouraging and functional climate, the leader must design the actual structure of succession. In too many cases, middle management is crippled by isolation. As people proceed up the ladder, they are enclosed by norms, beliefs, and values that are peculiar to middle management. When they finally get to the top, a whole new array of forces—environmental, political, economic, and financial—confronts them in forms they have never had to consider. For example, people who come up through the financial end of an institution are bookkeepers by instinct and training. But the vice-president in charge of finance is, or should be, adept at legitimate gambling and risk taking. Nothing in his or her prior experience as a bookkeeper, accountant, or steward of other people's money has prepared that person for the job he or she has been aiming at from the moment of joining the organization.

The leader should create a transitive organization, so that

job *A* prepares one for job *B*, which, in turn, prepares one for job *C*. In the bookkeeping-finance trajectory, the career line is intransitive. This linear but illogical sort of structure is the real basis for the Peter Principle: people inevitably rising to the level of their own incompetence. At the same time, the leader should incorporate a reflective arena into his or her structure, so that time out for musing is mandatory. I'm not speaking here of the sort of retreats that organizations have recently become so fond of, because they are usually the same old routine in a new locale. If people in authority stopped regularly to think about what they were doing, they would have the kinds of fresh insights they now pay consultants dearly for. As perspective is vital to the painter or writer, it is vital to leaders and their associates.

Both the culture of work and the structure of the organization must also contain intangibles, such as opportunities for everyone at every level to learn in order to maintain and improve job satisfaction, a stated code of ethics to establish and maintain honesty and probity, and the means to manage and resolve differences and conflicts. Conflict is inevitable, and it can be destructive or useful, depending on how the leader handles it.

There are two fundamental bases for conflict. The first is information. *Y* has information that *A* doesn't have, or, as sometimes happen, *Y* and *A* have completely different information. The second is perception. People simply see things differently. For example, marketing sees products differently from the way their designers do, or a Princeton graduate has a different perception of life from a retired Army colonel. Where one sits determines where one stands. In these general areas, the manager is apt to rush about, trying to encourage workers to learn, insisting that they be honest, and literally intervening in conflicts. The leader, on the other hand, has already created an environment in which opportunity, honesty, and a kind of automatic mediation device exist.

Leaders do not avoid, repress, or deny conflict, but rather see it as an opportunity. Once everyone has come to see it that way, they can exchange their combative posture for a creative stance, because they don't feel threatened, they feel challenged.

Henry Mintzberg (1973) named eight prime leadership skills:

1. Peer skills—the ability to establish and maintain a network of contacts with equals.
2. Leadership skills—the ability to deal with subordinates and all the complications that come with power, authority, and dependence.
3. Conflict resolution skills—the ability to mediate conflict, to handle disturbances under psychological stress.
4. Information-processing skills—the ability to build networks, extract and validate information, and disseminate information effectively.
5. Skills in unstructured decision making—the ability to find problems and solutions when alternatives, information, and objectives are ambiguous.
6. Resource allocation skills—the ability to decide among alternative uses of time and other scarce organizational resources.
7. Entrepreneurial skills—the ability to take sensible risks and implement innovations.
8. Skills of introspection—the ability to understand the position of a leader and his or her impact on the organization.

That's good, but there's more—an x factor that's quintessential. The leader knows what we want and what we need before we do and expresses these unspoken dreams for us in everything he or she says and does. When Martin Luther King spoke of his dream, for a moment, all of us, black and white alike, were one. Of course, now we are all wiser, and more cynical, and we don't believe in dreams anymore. But deep in all of us there is still and always a need to believe, and one day a leader will appear who will express that need, and fulfill it.

These are, as I've said, hard times for leaders, but true leaders are not deterred by hard times. That is perhaps, finally, what makes them leaders. As Abigail Adams wrote long ago to Thomas Jefferson, "Great necessities call forth great leaders."

Postscript

This postindustrial epoch is characterized by material growth, humanity over nature, competitive self-interest, rugged individualism, a belief that large is beautiful, specialized work roles, standardized products, and a generally stressful existence. We are defined by our patterns of consumption and work status, not by who we are but by what we do. Once we believed that success was achieved through hard work, frugality, industry, diligence, prudence, and honesty. Now we believe that success is based in our personality alone. If we can please other people, we will succeed. Instead of working at work, we work on our personalities. Instead of being good at what we do, we opt for charm. And we do not dream, we fantasize.

The country itself seems stalled in some kind of limbo. It is not going to either the left or the right. We are not becoming reactionary or radical. When we respond to problems at all, we respond ambidextrously: right, left, right, left. Perhaps a certain ambivalence is appropriate; remaining open to redefinitions is necessary, and admitting of a future that is unlike the past is essential. After all, as the guru of the Beat Generation, Jack Kerouac, said, "Walking on water wasn't built in a day."

Index